ENDORSEMENTS OF *

Billy Graham was quoted as saying, "a coach can impact more lives in a year than a pastor can in a lifetime." I've been involved in sports on every level for over 45 years, in sports ministry for over 20 years, and I've witnessed the impact and influence that a Christian coach has on their players and their fellow coaches! It blesses me to read these devotionals from coaches from one of my favorite books of the Bible, Proverbs. Stewart Hardy, of All In Sports Outreach, has done a great job of assembling these devotionals from coaches all over the country. They are very applicable and I'm looking forward to sharing these nuggets of wisdom with our coaches and players during our #ProverbsChallenge in the months of January, May, and October each year.

JOHNNY SHELTON
Team Chaplain
Baltimore Ravens

The coaching profession, or ministry as I like to call it, is so much bigger than X's & O's, wins & losses, and chasing rings. It's about leading & influencing young people beyond the arena of competition and into the game of life. The "All-In: 31 Days in Proverbs" is a daily devotional written for coaches by coaches. I pray the wisdom extracted from the Proverbs, coupled with personal testimonies, both refresh and encourage you as you walk out and fulfill your calling on the greatest mission field in the world.

MIKADO HINSON
Director of Player Development
Texas A&M Football

I love the vision behind this project from Stewart Hardy and All In Sports Outreach. It's not all about "big names" (although there are some included), but instead about coaches of all levels digging into the wisdom of Proverbs and sharing what they're learning with the rest of us. This is a great example of the Christian life in action: experienced both individually and in community.

PAUL EMORY PUTZ, PH.D.
Assistant Director, Faith & Sports Institute
Baylor University's Truett Theological Seminary

ALL IN

31 DAYS IN PROVERBS

———

ALL IN SPORTS OUTREACH

All In: 31 Days in Proverbs
©2021 by All In Sports Outreach
allinsportsoutreach@gmail.com

All rights reserved. No part of this publication may be reproduced, stored in a retrieval system, or transmitted in any form or by any means—electronic, mechanical, photocopy, recording, or otherwise—without prior written permission of the author. The only exception is brief quotations in printed reviews.

All Scripture quotations, unless otherwise indicated, are taken from The Holy Bible, English Standard Version®, (ESV®), Copyright © 2001 by Crossway, a publishing ministry of Good News Publishers. Used by permission. All rights reserved.

Scripture quotations marked NIV are taken from The Holy Bible, New International Version® NIV® Copyright © 1973 1978 1984 2011 by Biblica, Inc.™ Used by permission. All rights reserved worldwide.

Cover and Interior Design: Abby Grace Meads
www.teammeads.com

A SPECIAL THANK YOU TO ALL WHO CONTRIBUTED TO THIS PROJECT:

———

STEPHEN BACA

PAUL BREITBACH

DERRICK BROTHERS

STEPHEN BYRD

BO CAMACHO

JEFF CONAWAY

RAMONE CONLEY

SPENCER CRACE

DANIEL FOSTER

VERNON FOX III

JESSE FRISINGER

SCOTT JACKSON

ALEX JOHNSON

BOBBY LEIDNER

CHRIS MELSON

BEN PIKE

TOMMY POYNTER

MICHAEL PRESELY

CREIGHTON REED

SEAN RILEY

RYAN ROECKER

LOGAN SIMMONS

TANNER SWINFORD

KERI TIMMERMAN

TRISTAN WEBER

CONTENTS

———

A LETTER FROM THE PRESIDENT/CO-FOUNDER

———

Proverbs 27:17 says; "Iron sharpens iron, and one man sharpens another. " This devotional was birthed from that verse and closely aligns with our mission to encourage coaches, athletes, and neighborhoods in their walk with Christ. I cannot think of a better way to live out that mission than 31 days in the Book of Proverbs and these devotionals written by your peers in the coaching profession for you.

We all seek to gain more knowledge and wisdom which begins only in The Word of God. The Book of Proverbs is full of wisdom to assist us in our daily lives. Our desire is for you to draw daily application as you read through the Proverbs, whether alone or in a small group.

Continue to seek wisdom and to know Him through The Word. Never stop living ALL IN for Him!

STEWART HARDY
President/Co-Founder
All In Sports Outreach
www.allinsportsoutreach.org

PROVERBS 1

STEPHEN BACA
Director of Operations, Performance Course
Dallas, TX

KEY VERSE: v.7, v.10, and v.33

THE FEAR OF THE LORD IS THE BEGINNING OF KNOWLEDGE, BUT FOOLS DESPISE WISDOM AND INSTRUCTION.

MY SON, IF SINNERS ENTICE YOU, DO NOT CONSENT.

BUT WHOEVER LISTENS TO ME WILL DWELL SAFELY, AND WILL BE SECURE, WITHOUT FEAR OF EVIL.

Do you know the difference between knowledge and wisdom? Knowledge, like most things, is great to have but is useless unless it is applied! Wisdom is the practical application of things that we know. Knowledge tells us how financial systems work while wisdom is managing a budget properly. Thankfully, we have the wisest man to ever live, Solomon, writing us a book of knowledge and practical wisdom inspired by a God who is the beginning of both. If we have any interest in obtaining this incredible fountain of practical advice we must understand first and most importantly that none of it can be gained with human effort, energy, or ingenuity. The only way these lessons are available and profitable to us is through a right relationship with our creator. The vertical flow of love and pursuing a relationship with our Father will in turn flow horizontally out from us and impact our thoughts, words, decisions and relationships. When we build our foundation on our relationship with God we can stand upright and immovable, regardless of what storms or trials may come our way!

The first checkpoint in Proverbs 1 is to ask yourself if your relationship with God is the main priority and ultimate desire of your life. If it is not, like a tree planted in the desert, most everything else growing from you will eventually wither and ruin.

What do we come to next? It is interesting to note that as Solomon is preparing to write a book 31 chapters long about practical life, he begins with warning us against the company we are keeping. It is said "show me your friends and I will show you your future." Surrounding ourselves with people who are not chasing after the same things as we are, primarily a passionate relationship with Christ, is setting us up for failure! We must take an inventory of the qualities of the people we are spending the most time around. We all know that the most effective kind of pressure is peer pressure! If we are around it, we will likely become it. We have already established that human effort alone will not be our saving grace, that kind of strength comes from the Lord alone. Thus, if we are hanging out with evil, we can expect evil to infect us.

The development of discernment and wisdom take time, it is a process to learn how to live life like Christ, one that will be ongoing until we are perfected and with Him in eternity. Solomon portrays wisdom as a woman who is loud and visible, calling out for anyone who wants her to have her. If her cry isn't heard, how loud are the distractions around us? Foolish people, according to Solomon, not only spend time with people that lead them away from righteousness but try to call on wisdom when their paths reach the forewarned destruction. When we fall flat on our face and run from righteousness, we have only ourselves to blame, the wisdom begins at the fear of God and is screaming out to us all along the way!

In our life, we will reap the harvest for which we sewed. If we ignore the necessity to prioritize a relationship with our creator, it will make it difficult to hear wisdom cry out to us amidst the noise and the evil that surrounds us. Don't be a fool, we will get the proper return on our investments! We were created by God who passionately loves us and desires to have a personal and intimate relationship with us! We are not perfect and will never be, but if we daily remind ourselves what we are living for, God tells us that we will live safely, peacefully, and without the fear of evil. Lean into that relationship today and surround yourselves with others who have the same mission!

REFLECTION QUESTIONS:

Is the priority of my life pursuing an intimate relationship with God?

What are the things in my life that are so loud and are drowning out the cries of God's wisdom?

Do the people that I spend the most time with possess the qualities of the person I want to be? Do they, more importantly, possess the qualities of the person God wants me to be?

PRAYER:

Father, I pray today that you would allow my mind to understand that everything begins and ends with you. My relationship with you is my number one priority and I ask you to drown out the evil around me that tries desperately to keep me from hearing your call. Help me to surround myself with people who love you and will point me to you rather than drag me away. Give me the safety and the peace that comes from putting you in the center of my life. I will not fear evil because you are on my side. In your son Jesus' name I pray, Amen.

RESPOND:

Write down your own thoughts, observations, application points and/or prayers.

_____

_____

_____

_____

_____

_____

_____

_____

_____

_____

_____

_____

_____

_____

_____

_____

_____

_____

_____

_____

_____

_____

_____

_____

_____

_____

_____

PROVERBS 2

JEFF CONAWAY
Athletic Director/Head Football Coach — Shiloh Christian
Springdale, AR

KEY VERSE: v. 4-5

IF YOU SEEK IT LIKE SILVER AND SEARCH FOR
IT LIKE HIDDEN TREASURE, THEN YOU WILL
UNDERSTAND THE FEAR OF THE LORD AND
DISCOVER THE KNOWLEDGE OF GOD.

We have all wondered the worth of certain things throughout life.
As a child it may have been the worth of a baseball card, a piece
of jewelry, or the value of our dream vehicle. As we age, we are
interested in the worth of a home, a stock option, or the worth of
a business deal. In the second chapter of Proverbs, we see just
how valuable "wisdom" really is. More than that, we discover how
to gain wisdom and also the rewards that come with it.

The writer (King Solomon) begins the chapter with a very intimate
address to someone he loves and cares deeply about. He starts
with, "My son" and we can quickly understand the importance
and urgency of what must be coming next and how we should
receive this "fatherly" advice. He continues with one of the
most meaningful "if/then" sequences in all of scripture. If you
do this, then you can expect this. As a coach, we live in these
if/then situations. If our athletes commit to our most important
components of our team, then they will improve and position
themselves to achieve success.

Proverbs states that if we seek wisdom like silver and search
for it like hidden treasure, then we will be able to understand
the fear of the LORD and discover the knowledge of God. This
"wisdom's worth" is far more valuable than baseball card, piece
of jewelry, property, or any other thing this world can offer. For

the LORD gives wisdom; from His mouth come knowledge and understanding. He stores up success for the upright; He is a shield for those who live with integrity so that He may guard the paths of justice and protect the way of His loyal followers.

This is sometimes challenging given the world that we live in. This takes time, effort, and energy. Many times, our lives are so full of tasks, noise, and distractions that we fail to properly pursue this incredibly valuable wisdom. We may further our education, become experts in other fields, read and study other topics, but totally neglect to search and find the wisdom that we all truly need. This is a very sad reality for many people and even many Christ followers, but we can change this. When we make up our minds that this wisdom is valuable enough to seek like silver and search for it like hidden treasure, then God will allow us to understand the fear of the LORD and discover the knowledge of God.

I think there are some very tangible applications to this biblical truth. I believe our seeking and searching can be most maximized with a simple plan and a commitment to consistency. I would like to present a Proverbs challenge that is guaranteed to bring value in our search for wisdom.

First, there are 31 chapters in the book of Proverbs. If you are in need of a reading plan, simply read the chapter with each corresponding day of the month.

Secondly, use the S.T.A.R. plan to begin seeking and searching. The STAR plan is a very easy way to dig into God's word and receive this wisdom and revelation from the Holy Spirit. He is our teacher and we need Him to teach us. The S in STAR reminds us to write the scripture. Write key verses down and spend some time processing. The T gives us an opportunity to write down our thoughts about those verses. What was the meaning when written and what are your thoughts about it now? The A allows us to write down ways we can apply the truth to our lives. How does this word of God need to be applied to me and my own life? And finally, the R is our response. Write your prayer responding to what the Holy Spirit just taught you.

Again, this is just a simple plan to make our study time more impactful and meaningful. As you seek and search for wisdom's worth, God will begin to show you invaluable things. You will want to write this down!

REFLECTION QUESTIONS:

Is this "wisdom" valuable enough for you to seek it and search for it?

If not, what in this world has your undivided attention?

Knowing the rewards listed in Proverbs 2, would you be willing to seek and search for this worthy wisdom?

PRAYER:

Father, thank you for uncovering your truth and your wisdom to us. As we seek and search for your wisdom, I pray that you would show us how we should think, walk, talk, and act. Please allow your wisdom to enter our minds, and your knowledge to delight in our hearts. I pray more than ever that discretion will watch over us, understanding will guard us and rescue us from the way of the evil. Store up success for us, your children, and be a shield for those who live with integrity. Protect us, your loyal followers. I pray this in the powerful name of Jesus, Amen.

RESPOND:

Write down your own thoughts, observations, application points and/or prayers.

_____

_____

_____

_____

_____

_____

_____

_____

_____

_____

_____

_____

_____

_____

_____

_____

_____

_____

_____

_____

_____

_____

_____

_____

PROVERBS 3

TRISTAN WEBER
Assistant Head Football Coach — Allen High School
Allen, TX

KEY VERSE: v.5-6

TRUST IN THE LORD WITH ALL YOUR HEART AND LEAN NOT ON YOUR OWN UNDERSTANDING; IN ALL YOUR WAYS SUBMIT TO HIM, AND HE WILL MAKE YOUR PATHS STRAIGHT.

When I was 4 years old, I memorized my first Bible verse. I can still remember the song that my Sunday School teachers, of which 2 of them were my parents, sang to help us memorize Proverbs 3. I can remember singing it in the car, at home, in the backyard, and all around the house. And while I still have no idea where they got the tune for the verse, it has stuck with me my entire life. "Trust in the Lord with all your heart; do not depend on your own understanding."

To the 4-year-old Tristan, memorizing this verse meant nothing more to me than getting the candy that accompanied successfully saying it on Sunday in front of my class. Now, as a grown Tristan, I can see what was going on in that class, those car rides, and bedtime routines. People all around me were investing time in the one thing that will never return void: The Bible.

I believe the Lord placed this verse on the hearts of my Sunday School teachers because of the way Proverbs 3 begins in verse 1: "My son, do not forget my teaching, but keep my commands in your heart" (NIV). The wisest man to ever roam the earth, Solomon, doesn't beat around the bush with this one: We *must* spend time in God's Word; storing it on our hearts, deepening our relationship with the creator of the universe. We must learn the heart of the Lord who IS love and grow from the teachings and example our Savior, Jesus, set before us when He walked the earth. And all we have to do is open up the Bible and start reading, plug in our headphones and listen to it read to us, or gather around with other believers and read it together. Get in the Word!

In my life, I have been blessed to have been surrounded by people who challenged me to get in the Word and memorize and store it in my heart. From my parents, to college roommates, coaches all around the country, and most importantly, my beautiful bride, Denisa. It is through these relationships I have learned one of the most important aspects of growing in our faith is the encouragement, accountability, and edification that comes from spending time with others who share a faith in Jesus. These people help keep us grounded when we are "wise in our own eyes" (Proverbs 3:7). They keep us accountable to "Honor the Lord with your wealth and with the firstfruits of all your produce" (Proverbs 3:9). And they are there to help steer us in the right direction when we "despise the Lord's discipline" (Proverbs 3:11).

I am in no way saying I am perfect or even great with memorizing Scripture, but I can personally attest that the ones I have put in my heart, God uses for His glory. This is my encouragement for all of us today; that we might show up every day, committed to preparing our "minds for action" (1 Peter 1:13), by spending time daily in the Word, and surrounding ourselves with others who will spur us on to a deeper relationship for our Savior! So, spend some time today reading through the wisdom in Proverbs 3. Listen for the verse(s) God is using to teach you something, and commit to memorizing that verse(s). It will make an impact on your life and the lives of those around you!

REFLECTION QUESTIONS:

What is a verse(s) that spoke to me at this moment in my life when reading Proverbs 3?

Who can I share this verse with to encourage/edify them?

Who can I ask to join alongside me in memorizing this passage?

PRAYER:

Heavenly Father, thank you for giving us the blessing of being able to read your Word, so we may learn more about you. As we commit to writing the Scriptures on our hearts, open our eyes everywhere we go for opportunities to share these Words. Bring people around us who will encourage us to dive deeper, as well as people whom we can encourage. May we live our lives striving to be more like your Son every day. In Jesus' name we pray these things, Amen.

RESPOND:

Write down your own thoughts, observations, application points and/or prayers.

_____

_____

_____

_____

_____

_____

_____

_____

_____

_____

_____

_____

_____

_____

_____

_____

_____

_____

_____

_____

_____

_____

_____

_____

_____

_____

PROVERBS 4

LOGAN SIMMONS
Offensive Coordinator — Elgin High School
Elgin, TX

KEY VERSE: v.13

TAKE HOLD OF MY INSTRUCTIONS; DON'T LET THEM GO. GUARD THEM, FOR THEY ARE THE KEY TO LIFE.

As a coach, have you ever told your players to not do something because you knew it would turn out badly? I'm sure we have all been there a time or two. A few years ago, in our last game of the season, we were playing a team with the area's number one kickoff and punt returner. This player had already returned close to 20 kicks/punts for touchdowns throughout the season. We told our kicker/punter all week not to kick it to that kid. Fast forward to the opening drive of the game where we were forced to punt. In the huddle on the sideline, we reiterated our message, "Do not kick it to #5." We snap the ball, and punt it.... right to #5. He then proceeds to take the ball 50 yards to the endzone.

In v.13, Solomon is talking to his son. He was urging him to listen to his words. Choose wisdom over wickedness. Light over dark. He was telling him to learn from his mistakes. In life, Solomon had drifted from wisdom, and fell into wickedness. He forgot to take God's instruction to heart. Taking to heart the instruction of wisdom will help you stray from danger in life. It provides you with the tools to withstand evil and to stay on God's path. We must continue to listen, learn and grow. Your life depends on instruction and wisdom. Although football is not a matter of life or death, that example provides us with a powerful message: follow instruction.

I often feel that, in that moment from the game, we got a little glimpse of what God sees. He gives us all of the tools for wisdom and guidance, only to see us do the opposite. Thank goodness He is a merciful and loving God! Brothers and sisters, take hold of God's playbook and follow the instructions that He has provided because they are the key to life.

REFLECTION QUESTIONS:

What instructions do you need to follow today?

How can following these instructions help you grow in wisdom and understanding?

How can you help someone else learn to follow the instructions God has provided?

PRAYER:

Father, I pray to you for everyone reading this. I pray that you would reveal to them the desires of their heart and help them to lean on your instructions. Help us to be grateful that, although we may fall often, you are a merciful, loving and forgiving God. I thank you for the "playbook" you have provided and pray that we would take your Word to heart. Help us to grow in you each and every day. In Jesus' name, Amen.

RESPOND:

Write down your own thoughts, observations, application points and/or prayers.

_____

_____

_____

_____

_____

_____

_____

_____

_____

_____

_____

_____

_____

_____

_____

_____

_____

_____

_____

_____

_____

_____

_____

_____

_____

PROVERBS 5

TOMMY POYNTER
Athletic Director/Head Football Coach — Wills Point High School
Wills Point, TX

KEY VERSE: v.3-5

FOR THE LIPS OF A FORBIDDEN WOMAN
DRIP HONEY, AND HER SPEECH IS SMOOTHER
THAN OIL, BUT IN THE END SHE IS BITTER
AS WORMWOOD, SHARP AS A TWO-EDGED
SWORD. HER FEET GO DOWN TO DEATH; HER STEPS
FOLLOW THE PATH TO SHEOL.

As men, when we read Proverbs 5, our minds can immediately go to the immoral woman and begin thinking of the dangers of sexual immorality, but I believe Solomon who was instructed to write Proverbs has more in mind than an adulteress.

We can easily give ourselves over to the worries of this world and forget what God has called us to do. The immorality of the woman in the Proverb can be equated to the immorality of our profession or a "win at all costs" mentality. The immorality of coaching can be an easy breeding ground for sin upon sin!

What we ought to do instead is protect what is holy! As Christians we ought to realize that without the person of Christ we are LOST, and that our relationship with Christ falls within context of marriage itself. We ought to always be enthralled with the wife of our youth, keeping the marriage bed holy. We commit to this when we get married and say "for better or for worse, in sickness or in health, until death do us part."

We need to remember that our ways are ALWAYS before God. If we think we are getting away with something, it will eventually come out, guaranteed. Trying to cheat or cut corners can get us into a lot of trouble, whether it is with the UIL, parents, kids or the law itself.

Finally, we must remember in the midst of a tempting situation that if we trust God, it will always go well for us. If we do not, we will most assuredly come to ruin, as the Proverb states. All life in sin leads to death, no matter how "good" it looks. All life in the Spirit leads to life!

REFLECTION QUESTIONS:

When you read Proverbs 5, what qualities of God do you see?

Whether you are married or not, what do you feel like God (through Solomon) is trying to say about the wife of your youth? What could the wife of your youth represent as it relates to Christ's relationship with the church?

What are the results that come without the Lord in coaching? What about results with the Lord? Have you trusted in God to provide you with everlasting life in the person of Jesus? What will you trust Him with in your coaching?

PRAYER:

Lord, help me to remember that without you I am nothing. God when I commit my ways to you, you will help me. Help me to steer clear of the immoralities of this world and let me drive right into your love. Forgive me if I have sinned against you by giving into temptation presented by immorality. Let me commit myself to my marriage, whether it be to my own wife or to Jesus and the church. I love you Lord. Amen.

RESPOND:

Write down your own thoughts, observations, application points and/or prayers.

_____

_____

_____

_____

_____

_____

_____

_____

_____

_____

_____

_____

_____

_____

_____

_____

_____

_____

_____

_____

_____

_____

_____

PROVERBS 6

SCOTT JACKSON
Missionary and Football Coach
Córdoba, Argentina

KEY VERSE: v.20-23

MY SON, KEEP YOUR FATHER'S COMMAND AND DO
NOT FORSAKE YOUR MOTHER'S TEACHING. BIND
THEM ALWAYS ON YOUR HEART; FASTEN THEM
AROUND YOUR NECK. WHEN YOU WALK, THEY
WILL GUIDE YOU; WHEN YOU SLEEP, THEY WILL
WATCH OVER YOU; WHEN YOU AWAKE, THEY WILL
SPEAK TO YOU. FOR THIS COMMAND IS A LAMP,
THIS TEACHING IS A LIGHT, AND CORRECTION AND
INSTRUCTION ARE THE WAY TO LIFE.

As a coach or an athlete, you know far too well about setting goals and achieving them. With each season comes a new goal, a point you are trying to get your team to. In order to get there, a lot of planning is involved—and then comes all the work of implementing that plan. If you are to be successful, you must think about large scale things such as creating a positive culture and competitive environment, and also on small, minute details, such as which type of defense you will run against a specific opponent. You will be especially careful to instruct your athletes to avoid making the big mistake that could cost the team the season.

In Proverbs 1-7, we repeatedly see the words "my son," and we can infer that this is a passionate parent who wants to see his children succeed at life. Like a coach with an end goal in mind, Solomon has an end goal in mind, yet he knows that he must give the proper instructions and leadership in order for his loved ones to get there.

In Proverbs 6 we see instructions on not binding ourselves in a contract too quickly (v.1-5), about being a diligent worker (v.6-11), the ways of those who do not follow God (v. 12-19), and warnings against going after an indecent woman (v.24-35). These are all specific teachings, similar to game-day instructions. However, in verses 20-23 we see the overall heart behind these instructions: to guide one to a good life.

If you are a parent, the most valuable thing God has trusted you with is not your job or your team, but the soul of your child. In order for you to succeed in your role to point them towards Christ, you need to have a plan, and end in sight, and then you need to put that plan into action.
As parents, the most important legacy we can leave is a generation that knows and loves the Lord.

Regarding legacy, Psalm 78:4 says "we will tell the next generation the praiseworthy deeds of the LORD, his power, and the wonders he has done" (NIV). And in Psalm 145:4 "One generation will commend your works to another, they will tell of your mighty acts" (NIV).

This world will throw all kinds of pressures, temptations, conflicts, and lies to our youngsters. A leader's constant Godly instructions and wisdom is what they need in order for them to come out as victorious. As Charles Spurgeon stated about this Proverb: "There are dilemmas in all lives where a guide is more precious than a wedge of gold."

Yet being a good guide will not happen by chance, just as we will not win a trophy by chance. We must be sure that what we are passing on is from God, and we will not be able to do that if we have idols in our lives before Him.

I think David Prince says it well for us in his book *In the Arena*: "Every decision we make regarding sports communicates to our children what we value as ultimate. Let us lead in such a way that there is no question we value the glory of Christ above all else, and let us lead the way Christ did: remaining personally present and available for our children. Faithfully teaching our children about the glory of the incarnate, crucified, and resurrected Christ demands time, patience, and presence."

Perhaps you are reading this and do not have children. Let me encourage you that you can still be working on leaving a legacy. If you are not pouring into specific lives currently, then seek out ways to do so. See how you may serve at your local church. Or perhaps identify a few individuals that you can start to develop a deeper relationship with. God is not looking for superstars with millions of followers, he wants you to be faithful with what he has given you and where he has placed you.

REFLECTION QUESTIONS:

How am I doing as a parent or leader at leaving a legacy? Do I have an end goal in mind?

Am I more concerned about my children's and/or player's performance, or their standing before God?

What are some specific things you can implement as a leader and teacher in order to take advantage of the short times you have with your children such as time in the car, or at the dinner table, etc.?

PRAYER:

God, help me serve you to the best of my ability. Thank you for giving me the opportunity to be a leader and to instruct others in the ways of the Lord. Thank you for giving me your Spirit to help me and for giving me grace when I fail. Help me to always keep the mindset of leaving a legacy so that when I reach the end of my life I will hear "Well done my good and faithful servant." May your Spirit be at work in those under my care so that they may heed my words and avoid a path which leads to destruction.

RESPOND:

Write down your own thoughts, observations, application points and/or prayers.

_____

_____

_____

_____

_____

_____

_____

_____

_____

_____

_____

_____

_____

_____

_____

_____

_____

_____

_____

_____

_____

_____

_____

_____

PROVERBS 7

DERRICK BROTHERS
Assistant Football/Basketball Coach — Coppell High School
Coppell, TX

KEY VERSE: v.1-3

> MY SON, KEEP MY WORDS AND TREASURE
> UP MY COMMANDMENTS WITH YOU; KEEP MY
> COMMANDMENTS AND LIVE; KEEP MY TEACHING
> AS THE APPLE OF YOUR EYE; BIND THEM ON YOUR
> FINGERS; WRITE THEM ON THE TABLET OF YOUR
> HEART.

The things we believe to the innermost depths of our hearts are apparent in our actions. If we truly believe the gospel, it transforms who we are and how we live. Keeping, treasuring, binding, and writing on our hearts the Lord's commandments means both inwardly and outwardly we display fruits of the Spirit.

This requires an authentic love for Jesus that develops a kind of "spiritual shape," (spiritual maturity) in us. For an athlete to be dynamic and effective he/she must be in shape physically and mentally. The same is true for coaches in a different light. We must continue growing and sharpening our skills in whatever we coach. Continuous time and energy must be put forth to achieve success.

This is similar to our walk with Christ. We don't strive for success and do good deeds to be "good enough," or to earn our salvation. Rather, we follow Jesus' example in how we walk. 1 Peter reminds us to be holy because He is holy. This is a call to excellence. Excellence is good ministry when representing Jesus wholeheartedly. Our love and affection for Jesus should spur us to long to be like Him. In doing so, we grow and develop, becoming spiritually mature or "spiritually in shape." An athlete who isn't in shape physically and mentally is more susceptible to injury, a liability, and undependable. Being "spiritually out of shape" leads us to being susceptible to the enemy, our own sinful desires, and a liability to those in our sphere of influence; this makes us undependable.

But God, who is the perfect coach, merciful and just, is quick to reaffirm who we are and get us back on our feet. Coaching us at all times, He builds us up when we feel torn down, and puts us back in the game even when we felt as though we were letting His team down.

REFLECTION QUESTIONS:

Before we can grow spiritually, we must assess ourselves and surrender any sin we may be harboring in our hearts. Is there anything in your heart that is holding you back from becoming "spiritually in shape?"

How can excellence be considered good ministry?

Why is it vital, not only for ourselves, but for those in our sphere of influence, to be "spiritually in shape?"

PRAYER:

Jesus, thank you for who you are, giving us the perfect example of what living excellently looks like. May our hearts be aligned with your will and all that pleases you. Let us strive to be spiritually mature to glorify you. Remove any things in our heart that are sinful, and refine us to become more aware of your Spirit who dwells inside us. Spirit, stir our affections for you and help us to hear where you are directing us. We love you, Lord, and are grateful you love us all the more. Amen.

RESPOND:

Write down your own thoughts, observations, application points and/or prayers.

_____

_____

_____

_____

_____

_____

_____

_____

_____

_____

_____

_____

_____

_____

_____

_____

_____

_____

_____

_____

_____

_____

_____

_____

_____

_____

PROVERBS 8

CREIGHTON REED
Offensive Coordinator — Odessa High School
Odessa, TX

KEY VERSE: v.11

FOR WISDOM IS BETTER THAN JEWELS, AND ALL THAT YOU MAY DESIRE CANNOT COMPARE WITH HER.

Proverbs 8 is all about true wisdom being found in Christ. Wisdom is a critical topic. Notice that wisdom is presented as a person and it gives us instruction on how to seek it. Proverbs 8:17 tell us to seek her, verse 32 tells us to listen to her, and verse 34 tells us to watch daily at her gates.

This reminds me of Colossians 2:3 which tells us that all treasures of wisdom and knowledge are found in Jesus. For HE is the one we seek. The "she" we see here in Proverbs 8 is now the "he" in Colossians and the second person of the Trinity. This chapter provides encouragement and lifts a weight off the shoulders of Christian men and women. In Jesus we have all the wisdom we need, can ever seek, and long for. Jesus is our wisdom treasure trove, as we follow Him all the days of our life here on earth.

Solomon tells us that wisdom calls us, raises her voice, takes her stand, and cries aloud, trying to get our attention. But it's a two-way street for us. Wisdom pursues us, and we are supposed to pursue the wisdom that is ours in Jesus. This wisdom is better than all our wins, gold, jewels, and records. Out of this wisdom we get knowledge, justice, discretion, and are better equipped to walk in righteousness.

Through wisdom we gain many advantages as a believer. Proverbs 8:32-35 tells us we are blessed, find life, and we obtain

God's favor. Not having wisdom will lead us to love death and sin (v.36).

The key takeaway is this: ALL the wisdom we need, for all the times we need it, and for all the areas in which we need it, is ours in Jesus Christ our Lord and Savior!

REFLECTION QUESTIONS:

In what areas of my life do I seek the jewels of this earth rather than the wisdom found in Jesus?

How can I flip-flop that and pursue Kingdom treasures rather than worldly?

PRAYER:

Lord God, thank you for providing all the wisdom and life we need in your son Jesus. We ask for your Holy Spirit to guide and direct us towards Kingdom treasures found only in you. Open our eyes to see those treasures and opportunities around us. Amen.

RESPOND:

Write down your own thoughts, observations, application points and/or prayers.

_____

_____

_____

_____

_____

_____

_____

_____

_____

_____

_____

_____

_____

_____

_____

_____

_____

_____

_____

_____

_____

_____

_____

_____

_____

PROVERBS 9

BEN PIKE
Head Football Coach — Fort Zumwalt West High School
St Louis, MO

KEY VERSE: v.10-11

> THE FEAR OF THE LORD IS THE BEGINNING OF
> WISDOM, AND KNOWLEDGE OF THE HOLY ONE
> IS INSIGHT. FOR BY ME YOUR DAYS WILL BE
> MULTIPLIED, AND YEARS WILL BE ADDED TO YOUR
> LIFE.

As coaches and former athletes, the idea of fearing something can be a bit foreign. Other than the occasional fear of failure, I have never entered a game as a player or a coach where I felt fearful of another opponent. We are taught to compete with no fear and to leave it all out on the field, so when the term Fear the Lord is brought up, it may sound a bit strange. As believers of Jesus, we know how great His love is, and if you are not a believer, you have most likely heard of the love of Jesus. So why then would I fear something that loves me and that I am supposed to love in return?

In the Bible, fear of the Lord has multiple meanings. First, it can mean judgement and wrath of God. Because of our sin, we will receive God's judgement, and we deserve his wrath. I often hear the saying, "Only God can judge me." While this is true, it should absolutely terrify us. Since God is the perfect judge, He will give the perfect judgement. Do you really want someone who is a perfect judge judging your life? Probably not. Praise God for His mercy that protects us from the fate which we deserve.

Secondly, fear of the Lord means having complete awe and reverence for Him. It leads to wisdom, which results in obedience. When you fear the Lord, you obey the Lord not out of obligation, but because you have such reverence, awe, and love for Him. Fear of the Lord may be one of the most significant things that is missing from the American Christian Church today. Many people see God as all love, however that is just one characteristic of God. By saying God is just love, we put Him into a box and limit Him to our understanding. Without fear of the Lord, we miss out on many other characteristics of God such as justness, mercifulness, holiness, faithfulness, omniscience, omnipotence, and so much more.

Fear of the Lord may sound negative, but it is actually positive and leads to wisdom. Fear of the Lord keeps us from falling to our temptations and prompts us to do what is right. When you fear the Lord, you gain wisdom, which puts you in God's will. This wisdom leads to obedience of God's commandments. Through this process, God's will becomes your own, and you can begin to see the true awesomeness of God.

Fear of the Lord leads to wisdom and through that wisdom, our days will be many and years will be added to our lives. Following the wisdom of God is the perfect blueprint for living a long and prosperous life. This in itself is not an ironclad promise. There are plenty of wise, God-fearing people whose lives are cut short in our perspective. However, when we have a relationship with Jesus, we have the ability to live life to its fullest because of His love. We must also look at this verse through the lens of eternity. Fear of the Lord leads to wisdom and God's grace. When His grace is upon us, we are promised eternity with Him. If we want a life full of wisdom, we must learn to fear the Lord.

REFLECTION QUESTIONS:

How can you model fear of the Lord to your players?

How often do you pray for wisdom and discernment?

In your life, how have you seen wisdom lead to obedience?

PRAYER:

Heavenly Father, I ask you to give me a humble heart that I may be in awe and have reverence of you and your holiness. I ask that your wisdom be poured out on me and that wisdom may lead to obedience of your word. Make your will my own that I may live a life that is full of love and that is glorifying to you. It is in Jesus' name I pray. Amen.

RESPOND:

Write down your own thoughts, observations, application points and/or prayers.

_____

_____

_____

_____

_____

_____

_____

_____

_____

_____

_____

_____

_____

_____

_____

_____

_____

_____

_____

_____

_____

_____

_____

_____

PROVERBS 10

BEN PIKE
Head Football Coach — Fort Zumwalt West High School
St Louis, MO

KEY VERSE: v.12

> HATRED STIRS UP CONFLICT, BUT LOVE COVERS
> ALL WRONGS.

As coaches, we have one of the best jobs in the world. We get to positively affect and love young people. There is nothing that can tear an individual, a family, a team, a community, or a country apart faster than hate. Ephesians 4:31 states, "Let all bitterness and wrath and anger and clamor and slander be put away from you, along with malice." We should protect our hearts at all cost from hate, and the only way to do that is to fill our hearts not just with love but with Godly love.

The Bible talks repeatedly about love; it is the main overarching theme of the gospel. For example, John 3:16 states, "For God so LOVED the world that he gave his only Son, that whoever believes in him should not perish but have eternal life." In addition to John 3:16, 1 Corinthians 13 touches all the different characteristics of love: "it is patient, kind, not envious, not boastful, not arrogant, rejoices in truth, bears all things, and endures all things." Without love we have nothing.

However, what is the difference between a worldly love and Godly love? Worldly love is typically rooted in pride, specifically how someone or something makes us feel or what someone can do for us. If it makes us feel good then we love it; if it doesn't then we don't. Worldly love is self-centered and will eventually lead to division. On the other hand, Godly love is completely the opposite. It's solely focused on other individuals, without wanting anything in return. How can I serve them? How can I lift them up? How do we love people that can do nothing for us?

Godly love covers up wrongs. Love is easy when the other person loves you and treats you in a way that you like to be treated. Where it gets difficult is how to love someone when they have wronged you, hated you, or have hurt you. God calls us to love and forgive all people, not just those we like. We must be willing to love and forgive those who have deeply hurt us. Luke 6:27-28 states, "But I say to you who hear, Love your enemies, do good to those who hate you, bless those who curse you, pray for those who abuse you." Repeatedly the Bible tells us that we must love those who hate and hurt us. This is not an easy thing to do, but we must do it because that is what Jesus did for us.

When we sin against God, we are committing cosmic-sized treason against the creator of the universe. We are saying, "God I know better than you, so I am going to do things my own way, I don't need you." This hurts God on a level that we can't comprehend. Despite our rejection of Him, God loves us so much that He gives us a way to salvation that we can choose to accept. He sent his son Jesus to take our place on the cross so that our sins may be forgiven, and we can spend eternity with God in heaven. We can do nothing for God, and He doesn't need us. He just wants to share His holiness with us. Even though we continually sin against Him, His promise of salvation remains steadfast through faith and grace. That is what Godly love looks like.

As coaches, we all have that aggravating player or challenging parent. How do we treat them? If we have Godly love in our hearts, we need to show those kids even more love; they need it the most. We must be willing to give grace to those that may not deserve it, because neither do we. God gives us grace because of His perfect love.

REFLECTION QUESTIONS:

How do you show your players you love them?

Do you tell your players that you love them? If yes, why? If no, why not?

How do you love the player that is "difficult"?

How do you help build love between your players?

PRAYER:

Heavenly Father, I ask that you protect my heart from hate. Do not allow me to fall into a pitfall that leads to destruction. Instead, fill my heart with your love that I may love others the way I love myself. Give me the courage to be able to use that love to forgive all those who have wronged me because you first forgave me. It is in Jesus' name I pray. Amen.

RESPOND:

Write down your own thoughts, observations, application points and/or prayers.

_____

_____

_____

_____

_____

_____

_____

_____

_____

_____

_____

_____

_____

_____

_____

_____

_____

_____

_____

_____

_____

_____

_____

_____

_____

PROVERBS 11

CHRIS MELSON
Former Athletic Coordinator/Head Football Coach
Sulphur, OK

KEY VERSE: v.2 and v.14

WHEN PRIDE COMES, THEN COMES DISGRACE, BUT WITH THE HUMBLE IS WISDOM.

WHERE THERE IS NO GUIDANCE, A PEOPLE FALLS, BUT IN AN ABUNDANCE OF COUNSELORS THERE IS SAFETY.

Proverbs is a wonderful collection of wisdom God has shared with us. If you read one chapter each day, you will finish the book in one month. Do that for a full year and you have filled your heart and mind with God's infinite wisdom 12 times over! You say you want wisdom and maturity—do this simple task and see where you end up in a year. Sometimes, we as believers, feel we don't need any more Bible reading. Maybe we think we've read it all and can't benefit by reading it over and over. That my friend is called PRIDE.

The first verse in chapter 11 I want to focus on is verse 2. This verse is true for all men in all walks of life. I really think it can apply to an assistant coach and his role on a staff. "When pride comes, then comes disgrace, but with the humble is wisdom." God is telling us that if we become prideful, we are certain to face disgrace. However, if we show humility, we will gain wisdom. Do any of you happen to know someone who knows it all? You know, the guy on the staff or in the office that can't be told anything. Those guys, over time, will most certainly face dire consequences for their prideful attitude. They will not move up or advance. Ten years will go by and they will be in the same or lesser role they were when you first met them. Most guys with pride will also sit around and tell you how the head coach or coordinator should be doing things. The sad thing is that their prideful attitude does not just affect a coach's career, but worse than that, his entire family.

As a head coach, it never ceases to amaze me that the one coach who needs to get better is the one who refuses to go to clinics or read articles or watch videos to improve. Guess what, they don't last long on my staff and ultimately face a certain amount of disgrace. On the flipside, that young coach that is always asking questions, going to every clinic, constantly spending time on his craft, always seems to move up. You can't keep a guy like that from advancing. It may be even more impressive for an older coach to hang onto that attitude throughout his entire career. He never thinks he knows it all, but constantly wants to learn and improve.

Jesus, the Lord of all and creator of the heavens and earth showed us the ultimate humility by laying down His life on the cross. If we truly want to be like Christlike, a Christian, we must continue to have humility. We should constantly seek the truth by studying God's word and at the same time continuing to study ways to improve in our profession as a coach.

The second verse is more applicable to a head coach or perhaps a coordinator. Verse 14 reads, "Where there is no guidance, a people falls, but in an abundance of counselors there is safety." There is a component of pride involved with this verse as well. I spent 13 years as an assistant coach before I became a head coach. I worked for all kinds of head coaches. The one thing I learned was that I felt more valuable and responsible when the head coach listened to my ideas and suggestions. Obviously, the head coach has the final say, as it should be. But, for him to at least acknowledge me and listen, always meant a lot to me. If he refused to listen, it was very frustrating and led to discontent within the staff. That's not good.

As a head coach, I feel my greatest asset is my staff. I begin each year by telling my staff that any success we have on the field will be because of the work and effort they put forth. They are the key to our success, not me! I have 10 other men on the varsity staff with me that I rely on for input, ideas, and self-checking. I feel that if we are going to be successful in the battle every Friday night, it takes guidance from my advisers to make the best decisions. Prideful leaders who won't listen may be worse than assistants who are prideful. I hope that whether you are an assistant or a head coach, the study of these 2 verses in chapter 11 will help you understand how important humility is for you to gain victory on the field and in life.

REFLECTION QUESTIONS:

Are you prideful in your profession? If so, what needs to change? What can you do to show humility in your profession?

Are you prideful in your faith? If so, what needs to change? What actions can you take that would allow you to show humility in this area? What needs to change?

What do you take away from verses 2 and 14?

What is keeping you from reading a chapter in Proverbs each day?

PRAYER:

Dear God, our prayer is that you forgive us when we are prideful in this life. Help us to have the humility we see in your Son, Jesus. Thank you for giving us wisdom through your word, the Bible. Help us to submit ourselves daily and commit to reading your word on a regular consistent basis so that our pride will subside and humility will form in our hearts and our minds! We love you Lord! Amen.

RESPOND:

Write down your own thoughts, observations, application points and/or prayers.

_____

_____

_____

_____

_____

_____

_____

_____

_____

_____

_____

_____

_____

_____

_____

_____

_____

_____

_____

_____

_____

_____

_____

PROVERBS 12

DANIEL FOSTER
Offensive Coordinator — McKinney Boyd HS
McKinney, TX

KEY VERSES: v.11 and v.24

WHOEVER WORKS HIS LAND WILL HAVE PLENTY OF BREAD, BUT HE WHO FOLLOWS WORTHLESS PURSUITS LACKS SENSE.

THE HAND OF THE DILIGENT WILL RULE, WHILE THE SLOTHFUL WILL BE PUT TO FORCED LABOR.

Many of us believe the harder you work the better you will be. In sports the person who works the hardest is the one who wins. In life the boss is usually the one who worked his way up that ladder and made it to the top with hard work and dedication. As parents we try to teach our kids to work hard for what they want, and once they do they will get it. My question is: Are we teaching our kids right? Are we telling ourselves what God word says? Are we believing that we will all get the prize at the end of the race, or are we saying the prize is the path you take to obtain the prize? "I press on toward the goal for the prize of the upward call of God in Christ Jesus" (Philippians 3:14). Proverbs 12 verses 11 and 24 gives us wisdom from King Solomon that helps us understand "HARD WORK." Let's go and see what he has to say.

Verse 11 states "Whoever works his land will have plenty of bread, but he who follows worthless pursuits lacks sense." The first part of the verse talks only about working and having plenty of bread. What I get out of this is that when you work you will understand how to obtain bread. It does not say you will have the best bread, or that you will have more bread than others. It just states you will have bread. We have a tendency of looking at God's Word and thinking we will become rich, or we will get what

41

we want. There are many times we take God's Word and turn it into what we want it to be, rather than making it what He wants us to be. Our Father wants us to be hard workers not to obtain a prize, but to help expand the Kingdom of Heaven. It's hard work to stay in the word daily, it is hard work not to sin, it is hard work training up a child in the way he should go, it is hard work preaching the gospel of Jesus Christ with your action and your words! When we develop the mindset of hard work for Christ we develop within us a heart for others, a fire within that will never be blown out. We will all have hard times come our way, the question is: have we worked hard to make sure our prize is having peace in Christ Jesus?

You might be asking: well, what if I don't work hard? What if I want to chase other things? I am glad you asked, because the 2nd part of the verse states "but he who follows worthless pursuits lacks sense." I am assuming that if you are reading Proverbs then you are looking for or wanting knowledge. If wisdom and knowledge is what you want then not working hard is not an option for you. As coaches we pride ourselves in outworking others, or being known as a staff who works hard. I ask you this: are you working hard to further the Kingdom of Heaven like you are working to become a state champion? If you are, then you are already on the path of gaining knowledge and understanding. If you are not, then decide today that you will match your professional work ethic with your walk with Christ. Say today that you will be ALL IN for HIM!

REFLECTION QUESTIONS:

What does Hard Work for the Kingdom look like in my life right now?

What does my practice plan look like for my sports? What does my practice plan look like for my God? How can I better prepare myself to be a Hard worker?

PRAYER:

Lord, today I ask you to help me in working hard for you. I ask that you allow me to understand the way of the wise and gain knowledge to become a hard worker. I know that the prize I am seeking has already been given to me with the death, burial, and resurrection of your Son Jesus. I thank you for your grace and mercy over my life. In your name we pray, Amen.

RESPOND:

Write down your own thoughts, observations, application points and/or prayers.

_____

_____

_____

_____

_____

_____

_____

_____

_____

_____

_____

_____

_____

_____

_____

_____

_____

_____

_____

_____

_____

_____

_____

PROVERBS 13

MICHAEL PRESLEY
Assistant Coach — Coppell Middle School East
Coppell, TX

KEY VERSE: v.6

RIGHTEOUSNESS GUARDS HIM WHOSE WAY IS
BLAMELESS, BUT SIN COVERS THE WICKED.

The word righteousness is used six times alone in this chapter, which begs the question, what exactly does the author mean by righteousness? The concept of righteousness is not solely regulated to this chapter of Proverbs, it is rampant in the entirety of Scripture. This gives even more credence to how significant righteousness actually is to the gospel narrative. Jesus Himself counts those blessed who hunger and thirst for righteousness (Matthew 5:6).

Righteousness, or to be righteous, is wording that is used quite often both in and out of the church. Perhaps it is used so much that we kind of lose its meaning. After all, if you were to ask 100 people what righteousness is you would almost get 100 different responses. In order to fully understand what is meant we need to unpack its meaning at it is used by the author of this Proverb.

The words righteousness and justification (or some sort of variations of these two words) are rather married throughout Scripture. They go together, even at some points interchangeable. If one is justified before God, they are made righteous before God. While there are some differences, they almost mean the same thing. To be justified, or to be made righteous, means to die to our old self and be brought into the family of God, more specifically to be adopted as sons and daughters into God's family (John 1:12; Romans 8:15). When we are justified, or made righteous, we are in the proverbial courtroom setting in which God "declares" us to be in the right, or part of His family now.

However, righteousness has an outworking effect. It is not merely a self-exclusive event; rather it is a person being declared righteous by God and therefore desiring to replicate that love to other people. That is to say, that to hunger and thirst for righteousness is to meditate on and absorb the love God has to offer and then go and replicate that socially to others. This is what is meant by "faith without works is dead (James 2:14)."

This brings us back to our focal verse for the chapter, "righteousness guards him whose way is blameless, but sin covers the wicked." Those who have been declared righteous by God are guarded, or protected. However, the one who indulges willingly in sin and wickedness will be covered by the dark cloud of sin. As coaches we have heard plenty of coachisms, or inspirational quotes to get the team going. One of the more popular coaching quotes is "you are what you repeatedly do." Meaning, what you consistently do ultimately defines who you are. If you are consistently mean and short with people in your neighborhood, you will get the reputation of a grouch among your neighbors. If you consistently are loving and kind in your workplace, you will get the reputation of a generous and jovial person among your peers. Same goes for sports. If you consistently work hard and win, you will be known as a coach or player who is a hard-working winner.

One who consistently walks in a blameless way, is covered by the righteousness bestowed onto them by God. However, the one who entertains and acts on wickedness is covered by sin.

REFLECTION QUESTIONS:

In what ways do ensure that you consistently walk in righteousness?

In what areas of your life are you walking in wickedness?

How would you answer the statement "you are what you repeatedly do" about yourself?

PRAYER:

God, we acknowledge you as creator or all things. You are the most powerful being, and you answer to no one. We revere you and all the things you have done. God, we confess that we are sinners, saved by grace. We fall short yet you have faithful patience and mercy for us. We are thankful that you have counted us as righteous. Thank you for rescuing us from the dark cloud of sin and transferring us into the light. Please give us the desire to go and act on that righteousness. May we love our brothers, and our enemies. In Jesus' name we pray, Amen.

RESPOND:

Write down your own thoughts, observations, application points and/or prayers.

_____

_____

_____

_____

_____

_____

_____

_____

_____

_____

_____

_____

_____

_____

_____

_____

_____

_____

_____

_____

_____

_____

_____

_____

PROVERBS 14

MICHAEL PRESLEY
Assistant Coach — Coppell Middle School East
Coppell, TX

KEY VERSE: v.2

> WHOEVER WALKS IN UPRIGHTNESS FEARS THE LORD, BUT HE WHO IS DEVIOUS IN HIS WAYS DESPISES HIM.

Fear is a common term in this chapter. As a coach, you have most likely used this word quite often, either directed to your players, or even directed to yourself. One of the most popular quotes of all time comes from FDR's inaugural address where he said "the only thing we have to fear is fear itself." The president was trying to put an end to the depression and was attempting to do so by changing the mindset of Americans.

How does this concept of fear play into our interaction with the Lord? After all, any time I think about fear, or even have a fear, it seems to be a negative response or emotion. However, I don't believe that is the response or emotion that is meant to be evoked in this chapter of Proverbs. The word used here for "fear" is used as something you're afraid of or something that you are in awe of. Different passages use this word "fear" in both ways, but they kind of mean the same thing. Think about the last major game or tournament you competed in. Perhaps on the opposing side was an all-state player, or a legendary head coach who seemingly had never lost. Odds are there was a small amount of fear in you. Fear or apprehension about the big game is not inherently bad. After all, fear can drive us to do some pretty amazing things.

Furthermore, the fear you had for the opposing coach/team/player was most likely a respectful fear. Meaning that you were not terrified of them as a person; rather, you had a tremendous amount of respect for them and their tenure, and possibly even aimed to be like that coach one day.

The two uses of this word throughout Scripture suggest that to fear something means to stand in awe of something and/or have tremendous respect for something, knowing that that something has superior power over you. Think about the feeling you get when you stand in front of a high mountain, or the vast sea. There is reverence for these things; however, there is also a notion that the mountain and ocean are superior to me, therefore I must treat it with complete respect.

It stands to reason that we fear the very One who created that mountain and that sea. Fearing the Lord is key when examining and walking in relationship to Him. In fact, it is a building block by which the rest of our faith is set upon. Proverbs 1 tells us that "the fear of the Lord is the beginning of knowledge." That is to say that properly acknowledging God as who He is, is the best place to start in our search for knowledge. This concept is even mentioned twice more in chapter 14 alone (26, 27). In order to properly walk in righteousness, we must first fear God. By fear, I mean we must properly acknowledge that He is superior to us in every way, and therefore deserves our utmost reverence and respect.

REFLECTION QUESTIONS:

Do you fear God, in the sense that you recognize that He is superior to everything and therefore give Him complete reverence and respect? Why or why not?

Do you fear man more than God? If so, why?

In what ways can you consistently practice putting God in this place of reverence?

PRAYER:

God, we acknowledge you as creator or all things. You are the most powerful being, and you answer to no one. We revere you and all the things You have done. God, we confess that we are sinners, saved by grace. We fall short yet you have faithful patience and mercy for us. We thank you that you are involved in our lives. We ask now that you would allow us to fear you over man. May we never be ashamed of the gospel.

RESPOND:

Write down your own thoughts, observations, application points
and/or prayers.

_____

_____

_____

_____

_____

_____

_____

_____

_____

_____

_____

_____

_____

_____

_____

_____

_____

_____

_____

_____

_____

_____

_____

_____

PROVERBS 15

JESSE FRISINGER
Head Jr High Football Coach — Cole Valley Christian School
Meridian, ID

KEY VERSE: v.1-2

> A SOFT ANSWER TURNS AWAY WRATH, BUT A HARSH WORD STIRS UP ANGER.
>
> THE TONGUE OF THE WISE COMMENDS KNOWLEDGE, BUT THE MOUTHS OF FOOLS POUR OUT FOLLY.

I was never the smart one. Or the good looking one. Or the most athletic one. But more often than not, I was the witty one, the funny one, the clever one. To this day, my ability to use words and turn situations from negative to positive using humor have become go-to tools in my teaching and coaching toolbelt.

But should this be seen as a help or hindrance? Am I using this ability correctly? Or am I simply taking advantage of people and situations for the purpose of self-glorification? I have to admit that my words have been used as weapons on the field and in the classroom. An opportunity to build someone up, especially a vulnerable student, has been lost when my answer was far harsher than it needed to be.

Two seasons ago, I was coaching our "B" team during a Fifth Quarter game. For those of you not currently coaching junior high ball somewhere that players are in short supply, a Fifth Quarter game is a twenty-minute running clock game where your lightly used players get to work ten plays of offense and ten of defense. No score is kept, but EVERYONE knows who wins and who loses. They are an opportunity for the coach to be in the huddle and help everyone get set up properly. They are awesome confidence builders for less experienced, oftentimes smaller kids.

I had a young man who had enthusiasm but lacked understanding of what his job as cornerback entailed. After trying unsuccessfully to get him straightened out, I yelled to my assistants, "GIVE ME SOMEONE WHO KNOWS WHAT HE'S DOING, _____ CERTAINLY DOESN'T!" If ever there was a need for headsets in junior high ball, that was it! I had just singled out a young man who hadn't been coached properly before being put in a situation where that would be glaringly obvious.

Was I wrong in my assessment? Nope. Was my approach, with my coaching voice on blast, wrong? Absolutely. In the days following, a team dad approached me to talk about how I handled that situation. He was angry! I listened to him and agreed that I was 100% correct in my thoughts and 100% wrong in my actions. From that point on, I made sure that my communication with coaches was done face-to-face as to not single out a kid.

My mouth definitely "poured out folly" in that situation. This was a teachable moment for me! I knew going forward I needed to apologize to the young man in front of the team. He was somewhat perplexed as he didn't take my words personally. But he went away knowing that I was truly sorry. And I came away from that situation truly understanding the power of my words. I did not get to choose how my audience took what I meant to say. So, I'll forever be much more mindful of how I speak.

REFLECTION QUESTIONS:

Have there been times when I've used my position as a leader to demean someone? If yes, have I made it right with that person?

How would God have me use my position as a leader to speak life into my athletes' hearts and minds?

PRAYER:

Father, thank you for the gift of words. May I always be mindful of how I use them and let me be a builder of men rather than a destroyer! May my words be true, but spoken always with a regard for what others hear when I speak them. Amen.

RESPOND:

Write down your own thoughts, observations, application points and/or prayers.

_____

_____

_____

_____

_____

_____

_____

_____

_____

_____

_____

_____

_____

_____

_____

_____

_____

_____

_____

_____

_____

_____

_____

_____

_____

PROVERBS 16

BOBBY LEIDNER
Defensive Coordinator — Highland Park High School
Dallas, TX

KEY VERSE: v.3 and v.9

COMMIT YOUR WORK TO THE LORD, AND YOUR PLANS WILL BE ESTABLISHED.

THE HEART OF MAN PLANS HIS WAY, BUT THE LORD ESTABLISHES HIS STEPS.

As coaches, one thing that we always tend to look at is what our next step will be. We are looking for that promotion, for the better situation, for that head coaching position. I would like to take this opportunity to encourage you with using these verses in Proverbs to know who it is that truly holds your future and in knowing that His plan is always best.

I have a section in the back of my Bible that I have labeled Faith Builders. In this section, I make a list of all of the times I have seen God answer major prayers in my life. Many of these deal with my future; be it relationships, blessings for my current situation or potential job opportunities. Over the course of my life, I can look at these Faith Builders and see time and time again, where God established my plans. His plan is and will always be better than anything I could ever imagine.

An example of a Faith Builder in my own life occurred in the summer of 2019. A goal that I have for myself is to become a head baseball coach at some point. I would love the opportunity to lead a group of young men on the baseball field and in life. My current situation was one of a varsity position coach in both football and baseball at a very successful program. A fellow coach and friend of mine was leaving our program in a move to a better position for himself and his family. The new school he would be working at had a head baseball position available to lead a notoriously successful baseball program that would require a move to central Texas. I applied, interviewed, and was offered the position and the opportunity to fulfill one of my career dreams. Due to a family emergency, my wife and I were not able to be together during this critical potential life altering decision. We prayed together over the phone, talked for hours on the trip about the pros and cons, and talked to friends and family about the opportunity that was before us.

When making a major decision, I think it is important to pray, meditate over the Word, seek wise counsel, and pray some more before being led the direction God wants you to go. I have made many difficult life altering decisions in my life and this by far was the hardest one I have ever had to make. Choosing where to go to college, previous job changes, and asking my wife to marry me were all "no brainers" for me. I anguished over this decision. I was going to let the AD know in the morning what my decision was and when I went to bed I still did not know what to do. I felt like I could not go wrong with either decision. Proverbs 16:3 says to "Commit your work to the Lord" and verse 9 says "the Lord will determine a man's steps."

Committing my way to the Lord to me means taking it to Him in prayer. That night, I prayed, "God, I am struggling. Show me where you can best use me. You know my desire to be a head baseball coach. I just want to be where you can shine through me and I can impact students. Please show me where you want to use me and give me peace about my decision." I had to totally trust and submit to God's plan and His will. The next morning, I awoke and knew God wanted me to stay in my current situation.

Since that decision, I have been provided so many opportunities and blessings at my current school both on the athletic fields and in the classroom. God is using me to impact my students and my athletes and I know without a shadow of a doubt that I am where He wants me. This does not mean that decisions we make with

God will always be without trials and tribulations. Ask Joseph when he spoke to his brothers in Genesis 50:20. But, if you do commit your ways to Him and allow Him to establish your steps, His plan for you will be way better than anything you could ever imagine.

REFLECTION QUESTIONS:

Read 1 Peter 5:7 and Psalm 55:22. Potential life changes can cause lots of anxiety when trying to make decisions. Who should we lean on in these instances?

Read Proverbs 3:5-6 and Psalm 119:133. It is easy for us as humans to try and make every decision on our own. Think about what kind of attitude we should bring before the Lord when making decisions. How can our sinful nature affect these decisions?

Does God only want our big decisions? Or should we try and lean on Him at all times?

PRAYER:

God, I am committing to you everything that I do. You know my heart and you know my desires. I want to be where you can shine through me and I can have an impact on my students and my athletes. Please show me where you can best use me for your glory and determine my steps. Your way is best. Amen.

RESPOND:

Write down your own thoughts, observations, application points and/or prayers.

_____

_____

_____

_____

_____

_____

_____

_____

_____

_____

_____

_____

_____

_____

_____

_____

_____

_____

_____

_____

_____

_____

_____

_____

_____

_____

_____

_____

PROVERBS 17

PAUL S. BREITBACH
Counselor/Assistant Football Coach — Iowa City West High School
Iowa City, IA

KEY VERSE: v.3 and v.22

THE CRUCIBLE IS FOR SILVER, AND THE FURNACE
IS FOR GOLD AND THE LORD TESTS HEARTS.

A JOYFUL HEART IS GOOD MEDICINE, BUT A
CRUSHED SPIRIT DRIES UP THE BONES.

In athletics, we talk about athletes having "a lot of heart" or "the heart of a champion." What does that mean? How do we measure the heart of an athlete? It is a challenge. Why do some have it and others do not? When I think about it, the word that comes to mind is confidence. Athletes that are confident have that little extra when it comes to crucial moments in the game. How do they gain that confidence? This confidence comes from practice, determination and discipline. This confidence is developed one day at a time, one rep at a time. It is developed through hard work. The great thing is every athlete can develop the heart of a champion.

The same is true when we talk about our spiritual heart; it all starts in our heart. As in our physical life, we must have a heartbeat. It is the same in your spiritual life. It all flows from our heart. What is your heart pumping out? What is your spiritual heart pumping out into your soul and into the world? When our heart is right, all is right. In an age when everyone is looking for a quick fix; our heart makes us whole and healthy. Our heart is an active process with our faith. We seek God; we seek the good in others. We need to be constantly seeking and searching for the blessings and the opportunities to walk in faith. The Word of God is the blood of our faith.

The beat of your physical heart, does it tire because of a lack of training? If your physical heart has clogged arteries, trouble is on the way. If we do not take care of the physical heart, our life can be shortened. Life is filled with many distractions that can make us neglect our physical heart. The same is true of our spiritual heart. Many things can clog our spiritual heart, the list is endless. Is it worry, fear, anxiety, anger, resentment laziness? The Devil works to clog our spiritual arteries, for our heart to harden and that we will turn away from God and deny Him.

What is the remedy to keep our spiritual heart healthy?
Our spiritual heart needs to be exercised, daily. His word is nourishment for our soul and for our heart. When we read, reflect, consume and live His Word we are strong and we have the strength and the stamina we need to wage our battle with the foe, the evil that seeks to thwart and destroy us. Just as physical exercise is easier when done with others, the same is true of our spiritual exercise. Even more so in our spiritual life. Scripture tells us in Mathew 18:20, "For where two or three are gathered in my name, there am I in the midst of them." We are called by faith to walk together and to strengthen each other. Our faith does not grow in isolation. Our faith cannot be lived in isolation. We need each other.

Even our Savior called and walked with others on His faith journey. Jesus said to His disciples, "Come, follow me." Jesus today says to us "Come, follow me."

Jesus calls us to have a joyful and joy-filled heart. Jesus' journey from Calvary to Easter Sunday is our constant reminder that we are assured by our faith that joy comes in the morning. Yes, we have our trials and tribulations. We will face challenges that will make us question our faith. However, our faith is stronger than our fear. Let us always live as Easter people who go forth to make disciples of all the nations. Let His joy shine through us to and for all we meet on our journey in faith.

REFLECTION QUESTIONS:

Do you have the heart of a champion when it comes to your walk in faith?

What do you do when your faith is tested?

What does it mean to have a joyful heart?

PRAYER:

God, you have called us to walk in faith. You have called us to be strong in faith. You have called us to walk together in faith. We ask for Your guidance to help us to daily strengthen our heart. Create a clean heart in me. A heart filled with the joy and the glory of God. A heart that sees others as God sees them. A heart that gives us the confidence to walk and boldly and courageously live our faith. We ask these blessings in the name of our Savior, Jesus Christ.

RESPOND:

Write down your own thoughts, observations, application points and/or prayers.

_____

_____

_____

_____

_____

_____

_____

_____

_____

_____

_____

_____

_____

_____

_____

_____

_____

_____

_____

_____

_____

_____

_____

_____

_____

_____

_____

_____

PROVERBS 18

STEPHEN BYRD
Defensive Coordinator — Kingwood High School
Kingwood, TX

KEY VERSE: v.2, v.4, and v.10

A FOOL TAKES NO PLEASURE IN UNDERSTANDING, BUT ONLY IN EXPRESSING HIS OPINION.

THE WORDS OF A MAN'S MOUTH ARE DEEP WATERS; THE FOUNTAIN OF WISDOM IS A BUBBLING BROOK.

THE NAME OF THE LORD IS A STRONG TOWER; THE RIGHTEOUS MAN RUNS INTO IT AND IS SAFE.

As a kid, I grew up at the baseball field. We played multiple games a week, and even on the odd days, we would find ourselves at the fields watching our other friends play. When we weren't watching, we were playing "cup ball" or king of the hill on a dirt mound next to the fields. Age didn't matter and all were welcome. Occasionally, I would talk a little trash, and one time, I may have bit off more than I could chew. One rather large kid didn't take too kindly to some of the things I was saying, and he came charging at me. I took off, dropping what was in my hands, toward my "safe space" and ran into the concession stand where my mom was volunteering. I propped myself up on a stool and asked how I could help, in hopes that my mom wouldn't kick me out. The kid stood on the outside fuming mad, waiting for me to come out. My words got me into trouble. While I laugh about the story now, it came to my memory as I read through Proverbs 18. Our words matter, and more importantly, what we take in ultimately matters more. Am I giving God's Word the authority necessary to become a fountain to others?

Proverbs 18:2 exposes the root of the problem in us: empty words come from an empty and self-centered place that is only concerned with expressing foolishness.

While I'd like to say that this only applies to unbelievers, the truth is that the tension still exists for believers of Christ. If we fill ourselves up with worldly thoughts and divisive topics contrary to God's Word, we inevitably spew words that produce a kid twice your size that wants to beat you up. Okay, maybe not physically, but when we fill up with non-edifying foolish nonsense, our words will lack the kind of wisdom that produces life and expose a broken heart in need of Christ. Solomon says in Proverbs 18:4 that the wellspring of a man's being is rooted in wisdom. Jesus echoes these words in Luke 6:45 "The good person out of the good treasure of his heart produces good, and the evil person out of his evil treasure produces evil, for out of the abundance of the heart his mouth speaks."

We reveal the depths of our heart with the words of our mouth. In John 4:13-14, Jesus tells a Samaritan woman "Everyone who drinks of this water will be thirsty again, but whoever drinks of the water that I will give him will never be thirsty again."

The same security I was seeking from my self-inflicted enemy at a baseball field, we all seek on a greater level from our troubles in this world. The solution to our inward emptiness and sin leads us to an action. Run. Drop what is in your hands and run to the source of life. The more time we spend dwelling with Jesus the more his words become a living well inside of us producing life giving words and wisdom. They bring healing, extend mercy, love justice, and display a humility of a person that walks in devotion with God.

REFLECTION QUESTIONS:

Have you used your words to speak harshly, foolishly? If so, repent of being prideful with your words. Ask specific people to forgive you - if necessary. Seek reconciliation with God and people. (Proverbs 16:24)

Dedicate yourself to Scripture memorization. Is there a group of people you have a Bible study with? Anyone that will hold you accountable? (1 Corinthians 1:10; Galatians 6:2)

Dwell (Psalm 27:4). What does your prayer time look like? Is there room for moments of worship and reflection that will stir and strengthen your faith?

PRAYER:

Lord, I know that apart from you my words are foolish and lack real power. I repent. I ask that your words would be a river of life in me and that my speech would bring you glory. Help me to realize my need for you in every moment of my life and to set aside the time that you deserve to examine me and fill me with your presence for your glory and my good. In Jesus' name.

RESPOND:

Write down your own thoughts, observations, application points and/or prayers.

_____

_____

_____

_____

_____

_____

_____

_____

_____

_____

_____

_____

_____

_____

_____

_____

_____

_____

_____

_____

_____

_____

_____

_____

_____

PROVERBS 19

PAUL S. BREITBACH
Counselor/Assistant Football Coach — Iowa City West High School
Iowa City, IA

KEY VERSE: v.20-21

LISTEN TO ADVICE AND ACCEPT INSTRUCTION,
THAT YOU MAY GAIN WISDOM IN THE FUTURE.

MANY ARE THE PLANS IN THE MIND OF A MAN,
BUT IT IS THE PURPOSE OF THE LORD THAT WILL
STAND.

If I could teach the world one idea, or ideal, or concept it would
be the art of listening. And an art it is. Listening is a great
challenge, especially for those of us with Y-chromosomes.
As men, we are taught to be self-reliant, independent, self-
determined; the list is endless. Being a great listener is typically
not on the list. Heck, many of us will not even listen to our GPS to
find our directions. God blessed us with two ears and one mouth.
I think there is a message in our creation. How much better off
we would be if we talked less and listened more to God and to
others.

Our lives would be much better and more fulfilled. We would
save ourselves some of the struggles, etc., if we still our words
and open our ears to listen. In today's world, most of us listen
while waiting our turn to talk. We all want to be heard. However,
we do not always want to listen. How can we ever transform our
world if we do not listen to each other? As coaches, have we
learned to listen to our student athletes? Do we give them the
opportunity to share their thoughts and ideas? Do we ask for
their input? Do we really listen to what they have to say?

It really began in the Garden of Eden. Adam and Eve did not
listen to God. Instead, they listened to the serpent. Instead of

being honest when God asked, "Have you eaten from the tree that I commanded you not to eat from?" They lied and blamed each other and the serpent. God gave them everything and He gave them one request: do not eat of the fruit from the tree that He had given them.

How well do we listen to the voice of God? If we slow down and quiet ourselves, we will be able to hear and discern what God is calling us to as our ministry. Again, as men, we are not very good or very practiced as listeners.

Do we have the humility as coaches to listen and follow God's plans and not our own dreams and desires? Coaches are used to being in control. We spend hours upon hours in planning. We make the plans for practice, we prepare for every scenario and then the game begins and we have to let go and let our payers play. We are kidding ourselves if we think we are in control. This is the way God looks at us. He trains us, and if we stay in the Word He lets us play in the game. He lets us choose our paths in life. Yet if we are wise and we are listening to God, our dreams and desires will be in harmony with our heavenly Father's dreams and desires for us.

Just as we want our student athletes to be successful, our Savior came to give us life and life abundantly. When our game preparation comes together in a beautiful performance, it is likewise beautiful when we are walking hand in hand with God and the path He has called us to as our ministry. Bloom where you are planted. Be where your feet are, be present and hear God in the quiet. When we listen to God and we seek wise council from others our lives become a wonderful and amazing journey. God's plans are always better than our own. He is the best GPS, but only if we listen, reflect and seek Him. As coaches we don't let our athletes make the plans for each week. We would never turn over the reins to our athletes. We ask them to trust us. God is our coach. Do we trust Him? Do we listen to Him?

REFLECTION QUESTIONS:

How do you find quiet time to listen to God?

Who are the people you listen to who comes to you for advice?

Are your dreams, desires and goals God driven or worldly driven? How do you know?

PRAYER:

God give us the courage, strength humility to listen to you. Help us to still our hearts that we may hear your pans for us. May our ministry as coaches bring glory and praise to you. May our ministry as coaches bring others closer to you. May we always measure ourselves not by the worldly scoreboard. May our pursuit always be our Eternal Home. In the words of St. Vincent de Paul, "Our business is to attain heaven; everything else is a sheer waste of time."

RESPOND:

Write down your own thoughts, observations, application points and/or prayers.

_____

_____

_____

_____

_____

_____

_____

_____

_____

_____

_____

_____

_____

_____

_____

_____

_____

_____

_____

_____

_____

_____

_____

_____

PROVERBS 20

TANNER SWINFORD
Running Backs/Head Boys Track — Rockport-Fulton High School
Rockport, TX

KEY VERSE: v.6

MANY A MAN PROCLAIMS HIS OWN STEADFAST
LOVE, BUT A FAITHFUL MAN WHO CAN FIND?

We live in a world in which we are constantly being overwhelmed by conflicting voices, each fighting for the devotion of our hearts and the attention of our minds. The world's wisdom counsels us to believe that the outcome on the scoreboard, the number of championships we win, or our ability to develop a game plan will ultimately determine the extent of our influence and the quality of our legacy in the lives of those we coach. Resounding above these sin-corrupted voices, we hear the voice of God, graciously exposing the foolishness of the world's wisdom and inviting us to feast on the all-satisfying wisdom of His Word.

In Proverbs 20, we are quickly confronted by the reality that our success as coaches isn't marked by our career win-loss record or tactical knowledge of the sport we coach, but by our embodiment of God's wisdom and our imitation of Christ, who is the wisdom of God (1 Cor. 1:24). According to the wisdom of Proverbs 20, the Christian coach is marked by:

A DEVOTION TO THE LORD IN ALL OF LIFE (20:4)

Unlike the foolish, ungrateful sluggard, Christian coaches recognize that both the quality and extent of their efforts in this life are a direct reflection of their view of God. It is precisely because God is the sovereign Lord over all of life that the Christian coach labors and strives in all of his endeavors,

73

without exception. Due to their knowledge that God works in and through His people to accomplish His purposes, Christian coaches work heartily as for the Lord (Col. 3:23), and eagerly await the harvest.

A LIFE CONSISTENT WITH HIS PROCLAMATION (20:6-7, 11)

Too often there is a disconnect between one's proclamation, and one's lifestyle. In other words, it has become all too common among professing Christian coaches to talk the talk, but fail to actually walk with Christ as they practice and compete. While many coaches boldly proclaim the Lordship of Christ, most locker rooms are found void of obedient submission to Christ. In time, the reliability of our proclamation will be tested, and we will be made known not by what we say, but by what we do.

AN AWARENESS OF PERSONAL SIN (20:9)

The honest, self-reflective coach knows the extent of his heart's impurity and how desperately he needs to be cleansed from sin. The Christian coach acknowledges his failures to work heartily for the Lord and act consistently with his words, and recognizes them for the sins that they are. Beyond mere acknowledgement of these sins, however, the Christian coach will boldly approach the throne of grace with a penitent heart, knowing that, in Christ, he has an advocate with the Father (1 Jn. 2:1), and that God is faithful and just to forgive us our sins and to cleanse us from all unrighteousness (1 Jn. 1:9).

AN UNWAVERING TRUST IN THE LORD (20:22)

Finally, in whatever circumstance he may face, the Christian coach will confidently wait for the Lord and rest in His promised deliverance. When we become impatient and are tempted to doubt God's promise to deliver, we must train our hearts to remember that there is no loss too devastating, and no season too disastrous that God's promise will not prove faithful and true. How do we know? Because He who did not spare his own Son but gave him up for us all will also with him graciously give us all things (Rom. 8:32).

REFLECTION QUESTIONS:

What does laziness communicate about our view of God and how he works through the efforts of His people?

Why do you think the disconnect between the proclamation of the Christian faith and the practice of the Christian faith is so common among coaches and athletes?

How does the gospel transform our response to setbacks in sports and life?

PRAYER:

Father, forgive us for the times that we fail to submit all areas of our lives to the Lordship of Christ. Make us aware of the ways in which our actions are inconsistent with the words that we proclaim. Help us to trust in your promised deliverance, and rest in the redemption that we have in Christ. Amen.

RESPOND:

Write down your own thoughts, observations, application points and/or prayers.

_____

_____

_____

_____

_____

_____

_____

_____

_____

_____

_____

_____

_____

_____

_____

_____

_____

_____

_____

_____

_____

_____

_____

PROVERBS 21

BOBBY LEIDNER
Defensive Coordinator — Highland Park High School
Dallas, TX

KEY VERSE: v.31

THE HORSE IS MADE READY FOR THE DAY OF BATTLE, BUT THE VICTORY BELONGS TO THE LORD.

In the coaching profession, we have been entrusted with the responsibility of preparing and training our athletes for competition. In the secular world, our success is directly reflected on whether or not we win or lose that competition. We have a responsibility to prepare and train our athletes to be their very best at practice so that they can perform their very best in the game. We also have a responsibility to give them the tools, the game plan, and that chance to be successful each time they walk on the competitive field or arena.

I would like to encourage you to prepare and train them not only for their particular sport, but also for the game of life. I know that my calling as a Christian coach is to not only provide my athletes with the tools to be successful on the field, but to invest in their lives and let them see Christ through me. In order for us to be able to provide them with the tools they need in both areas of their lives, it is up to us to be the best version of "us" that they see. We must always be learning about our craft and ways to help our players succeed on the competition field. But more importantly, we need to be pouring over the Word of God, memorizing it and living it out each and every day. We should not expect our players to perform on the field if we ourselves are not prepared and fail to give them the tools they need.

We are all familiar with the story of David and Goliath and it is a great picture of the underdog fighting and winning versus one who traditionally would have dominated the field of battle. However, if we reread 1 Samuel 17, we find that David was never really the underdog. David was prepared and he was "made ready" through his young years as a shepherd walking with the Lord. His victory over Goliath on the battlefield was directly from the Lord. In fact, right before David slayed Goliath, in 1 Samuel 17:47 he says, "All those gathered here will know that it is not by sword or spear that the Lord saves; for the battle is the Lord's, and he will give all of you into our hands" (NIV). David's victory over Goliath rested solely with the Lord. The entire Philistine army and Israelite nation knew that the Lord was in control.

Proverbs 21:31 should serve as a reminder to us as coaches, that we should do everything that we can to prepare our athletes to be successful. However, we should not solely rely on our preparation for victory. Any success we see, comes directly from the Lord. And guess what, our defeats, they also come from the Lord. If God knows the number of hairs on our head, if He takes care of the sparrows, then I am sure He is in complete control over whether or not we win or lose a game. The good thing is that we can rest in that. Whether we win championships or don't win a game, God is in complete control over all of it. The only thing that we can do is prepare those we have been entrusted with to be successful. As mentioned previously, not only do we want to prepare them for their particular sport but also to be successful in their own daily lives.

Should God choose to bless you with victories and championships, thank Him for that blessing. Should God choose for you and your team to struggle in your season and not win a game, thank Him for those trials and the lessons learned. Should God choose you to be in one of the greatest professions in the world, thank Him for the opportunity to have an impact on your students and your athletes.

Take advantage of the opportunity that God has given you to be the best coach that you can be for your players. Strive to put them in the best situation possible to be successful, to prepare them for life.

Prepare your horses for battle, but trust God's plan for the victory.

REFLECTION QUESTIONS:

Knowing that God is in control of everything, what role can prayer play in preparing your players to be successful on the field and in their everyday lives?

Read Psalm 20:7, Hosea 1:7, and Isaiah 31:1-3. How do these verses reinforce the fact that God holds the victory in all aspects of our lives?

1 Corinthians 10:31 says for us to do all things for the glory of God. How can this verse along with Proverbs 21:31 be applied in our own life in raising our own children?

PRAYER:

Lord, you have everything under control. I pray that you help me and my fellow coaches to do everything that we can to help our players be successful. Help us to prepare them, invest in them, and to pray for them. We thank you if you choose to bless us with victories and we thank you if you choose to provide learning opportunities through failure. I pray that each one of our athletes will see you through us no matter the situation. You are awesome and we give it all to you. Amen.

RESPOND:

Write down your own thoughts, observations, application points and/or prayers.

_____

_____

_____

_____

_____

_____

_____

_____

_____

_____

_____

_____

_____

_____

_____

_____

_____

_____

_____

_____

_____

_____

PROVERBS 22

KERI TIMMERMAN
Wide Receivers Coach — Vandergrift High School
Austin, TX

KEY VERSE: v.17

INCLINE YOUR EAR, AND HEAR THE WORDS OF THE WISE, AND APPLY YOUR HEART TO MY KNOWLEDGE.

Preparing for one of our playoff games recently, walking back from practice during Christmas break I heard these words in my head. As I began to think on what that phrase meant, I reflected back to 1 Kings 19:11-13, where Elijah found himself hiding in the cleft of a mountain waiting on the Lord to pass by:

And behold, the Lord passed by, and a great and strong wind tore the mountains and broke in pieces the rocks before the Lord, but the Lord was not in the wind. And after the wind an earthquake, but the Lord was not in the earthquake. And after the earthquake a fire, but the Lord was not in the fire. And after the fire the sound of a low whisper. And when Elijah heard it, he wrapped his face in his cloak and went out and stood at the entrance of the cave.

This reminded me how often the Lord has spoken to me in a quiet moment, a sunrise or sunset, holding my three children while they slept. It reminded me that Christ so commonly makes his beauty, presence, and power known to us in these brief, quiet moments.

As I read Proverbs 22:17 again, I imagined a young child leaning in to hear a story or a truth presented by a father or grandfather, or coach. Patiently, observantly waiting to receive some beautiful piece of knowledge or training. It's so easy as fathers and coaches to miss these small, quiet teachable moments. It is also easy to use exaggeration or inflection or volume to emphasize a point. But here again God reminds us sometimes wisdom comes in a low whisper. Will we be attentive enough to hear it?

REFLECTION QUESTIONS:

How do you find yourself teaching your family and players most? Is it in the "low whisper," quiet, gentle leading or is it only through volume and the "strong wind"?

Are you leaning into God's word enough to recognize his "low whisper"?

PRAYER:

Lord help us to be those that lean in to find your wisdom. Help us to be the low whisper in our athletes and families lives. Help us to seek your wisdom and your words to share to a world constantly looking for a burning bush or a crumbling mountain for wisdom. Forgive us where we miss your still small voice and chase after having our own voices heard. Amen.

RESPOND:

Write down your own thoughts, observations, application points and/or prayers.

_____

_____

_____

_____

_____

_____

_____

_____

_____

_____

_____

_____

_____

_____

_____

_____

_____

_____

_____

_____

_____

_____

_____

_____

PROVERBS 23

BO CAMACHO
Assistant Head Football Coach/Defensive Coordinator — Hillcrest High School
Dallas, TX

KEY VERSE: v.15-16; 26

MY SON, IF YOUR HEART IS WISE MY HEART TOO
WILL BE GLAD.

MY INMOST BEING WILL EXULT WHEN YOUR LIPS
SPEAK WHAT IS RIGHT.

MY SON, GIVE ME YOUR HEART, AND LET YOUR
EYES OBSERVE MY WAYS.

Anyone who has been in the athletic arena knows that it takes a lot of "grit and grind" to be a champion! To be the best, it takes a lot of Great Outstanding Discipline (G.O.D.) and training. But it cannot happen without a great mindset and a passionate heart.

Our Father God is passionate about His people! He loves his sons and daughters so much that He gave His only begotten Son, Jesus to die for us. Wisdom can only be gained and obtained by knowing and walking with our loving and wise Father and giving our heart over to Him. The world will try to make us think we are wise and smart with our educational degrees or successful business ventures or worldly possessions, but that is a false sense of wisdom and success. In our Father's eyes, "true-success" is loving, living and serving Him daily when we love our neighbors and speak life-encouraging words to build them up and not tear them down.

When I was a child, I would mimic my two favorite athletes, Walter Payton and Gayle Sayers, and try to run and move like they did on the football field. They would slip and juke 2-3 defenders and spin away from them like they were ghosts... and off to the end-zone for a touchdown!

Well, shouldn't we observe and mimic our loving Father, through the example of His Son Jesus too? Our will should be to please Him daily and do His will. His Spirit is within us! His power, His glory, His goodness and His love run in our DNA! Let us be His hands and feet at work when we are at our workplace, our schools, our families, our students and our teams.

Be like your heavenly Father and see Him rejoice with joy! Seek Him daily and Be a Champion!

REFLECTION QUESTIONS:

How do you think God rejoices when we practice spiritual wisdom?

When our mouths are filled with His Word, how much joy do we bring to God when we speak the "Right Things?"

How is your "heart condition?" Is your heart filled with God and His love?

Do your actions line up with your heart condition?

Are you willing to listen to His good instruction and follow Him? If so, start today!

PRAYER:

Dear Father, thank you for your Son Jesus. It is my desire to worship and honor you Lord with all my heart so that you may rejoice in your son. Lord, I give you my heart so I can walk like you, talk like you and be like you. May your ways be my ways and your words of wisdom speak through me as I share your word with everyone I cross paths with in this life. Lord, lead my life to do your will so that I may put a smile on your face daily and do what is good and pleasing to you Father. Make Me A Champion, like you. Amen.

RESPOND:

Write down your own thoughts, observations, application points and/or prayers.

_____

_____

_____

_____

_____

_____

_____

_____

_____

_____

_____

_____

_____

_____

_____

_____

_____

_____

_____

_____

_____

_____

_____

_____

PROVERBS 24

DERRICK BROTHERS
Assistant Football/Basketball Coach — Coppell High School
Coppell, TX

KEY VERSE: v.5-6

> A WISE MAN IS FULL OF STRENGTH, AND A MAN OF KNOWLEDGE ENHANCES HIS MIGHT, FOR BY WISE GUIDANCE YOU CAN WAGE YOUR WAR, AND IN ABUNDANCE OF COUNSELORS THERE IS VICTORY.

Although the war has been won, each day we face is its own battle. In order that we may experience success, continued strength and might is completely necessary. Moreover, having a team of advisors or counselors is essential in the pursuit of victory.

In the modern day in which we live, strength is mistaken for vain masculine qualities, and might (or power) is mistaken for how much control we possess. According to God's word, wisdom and knowledge are representative of our strength and might. Knowledge gives way for an understanding that, when applied in the form of wisdom, leads to a peace that is bent on confident expectation or hope. This combination of knowledge and wisdom lets us see past the momentary hardship to the glory that is to come.

As coaches, it is our job to continually sharpen our practical understanding of a particular sport. Furthermore, making decisions that will benefit the entire team is proper stewardship of the knowledge gained. In 1 Corinthians chapter 12, Paul reminds us that we were never meant to do these things on our own. We are all parts of the church, the body of Christ. It goes without saying, but there's a reason why teams are made up of multiple coaches who specialize in a certain area of a sport. Although a head coach may be exemplary in one area of a sport, his assistants may be exemplary in areas he lacks. Those assistants also serve a purpose in sharing responsibilities that would leave a head coach less effective.

As flawed human beings in the process of sanctification, we fall short regardless of the amount of knowledge and wisdom we possess. This solidifies all the more the importance of the counselors we surround ourselves with. Failure or losing is only a lesson in the wake of success to be experienced. The reality is we don't always bounce right back when we fall, and we need those who will shoulder our burdens and pick us up when that happens. Proverbs 11:14 says, "Where there is no guidance, a people falls, but in an abundance of counselors there is safety."

REFLECTION QUESTIONS:

To you, what does it mean to have strength and might?

How are you stewarding the knowledge/wisdom you possess?

What does the "team" of counselors look like that you've built around yourself?

PRAYER:

Lord, we thank you for who you are. We thank you for the ability to gain knowledge and use wisdom that you so freely give us. I pray we'd strive in gaining knowledge, not to please men, but to please you and you alone. Let us be good stewards of the knowledge/wisdom we have and use it to glorify your Kingdom. May we allow a number of advisors and counselors around us that will push us to be better, pick us up when we fall, and affirm our identity which is found in you. In Jesus' holy and perfect name, Amen!

RESPOND:

Write down your own thoughts, observations, application points and/or prayers.

_____

_____

_____

_____

_____

_____

_____

_____

_____

_____

_____

_____

_____

_____

_____

_____

_____

_____

_____

_____

_____

_____

_____

_____

PROVERBS 25

SEAN RILEY
Athletic Director/Head Football Coach
Flower Mound, TX

KEY VERSE 11: v.11, v. 21, and v.28

A WORD FITLY SPOKEN IS LIKE APPLES OF GOLD IN A SETTING OF SILVER.

IF YOUR ENEMY IS HUNGRY, GIVE HIM BREAD TO EAT, AND IF HE IS THIRSTY, GIVE HIM WATER TO DRINK.

A MAN WITHOUT SELF-CONTROL IS LIKE A CITY BROKEN INTO AND LEFT WITHOUT WALLS.

Coaches are leaders of men, women, and children; much like kings in the Bible, we are leaders of more than who is on our team. We must lead our coaches, players, and their families. I am an honest coach but a calculated speaker. I know how powerful words are because I have seen my sons empowered and destroyed by them. Thus, speaking life over and into our players is necessary.

Proverbs 25:11 states "A word fitly spoken is like apples of gold in a setting of silver." As a coach or leader, the words you say are strong and purposeful whether you realize it or not. The old saying "sticks and stones will break my bones, but words will never hurt me" seemed like a declaration during my childhood, but it is a false declaration as every word has the power to pierce the deepest parts of our feelings and cast a lifetime scar. When speaking to your team, you should always speak from love, not from anger. For instance, not break out in the heat of the moment to launch a demeaning array of words that pierce the heart of one of your players. Solomon writes, "a word fitly spoken." That does not mean you cannot correct your players or coaches. It is the words you choose that help them learn while feeling loved.

In sports, it is apparent that competition is becoming more heated than ever, with fans feeling obligated to berate everyone involved in the game. The act of such disdain has bled over numerous generations and is becoming more difficult to correct. I am reminded of the movie 42 about Jackie Robinson. Jackie is on the field, and young boy is so excited to see the professional baseball players, so he eagerly watches as they come onto the field. His dad begins yelling racial slurs at Jackie, and the son looks confused at first, then looks at his dad and begins to mimic the hateful words of his father. That moment changed that young boy's life forever.

In Proverbs 25:28 we read "A man without self-control is like a city broken into and left without walls." Think of all of the times your team members have made you so mad you wanted to scream. The strong man of God will wait on the Lord for guidance with his tongue rather than spout off hateful words that break souls. Having self-control is important in games as well. I recently learned that many of the fans at our football games watch my reaction to calls by the officials to determine their response. I am a calm leader who believes officials can be ministered to as well. Matthew 5:16 says "let your light shine before men so they may see your good work and glorify your Father in heaven." By remaining in control, you show Christ to the other team, fans, and officials. Too many coaches are all too often praising God on Sunday and cursing him and everyone around them on Friday night. Self-control is an exercised responsibility that God ordains us to have.

Imagine showing up to a game Friday night against your hated rival school, and they greet you with a red-carpet treatment. They provide the team meal, give you the best locker room, have refreshments for you at halftime, and even announce each player as they run onto the field. That would be an interesting sight to see. Although a bit extreme, Solomon is speaking of this in Proverbs 25: 21 "If your enemy is hungry, give him bread to eat, and if he is thirsty, give him water to drink." Hospitality comes to mind first when reading this verse. It is hard to believe Solomon is this superficial; the verse must have a deeper meaning.

Biblically speaking, the verse challenges us to feed hungry souls. Our team and community are starving for strong Christian leaders that exemplify Christ on and off the field. Leaders who stay strong in the Lord in the toughest moments and whose character rises when most expect it to fall. Feeding hungry souls can be done by anyone reading this devotional. God has given us the power to spread the gospel. Matthew 28: 19-20 says, "Go therefore and make disciples of all nations, baptizing them in the name of the Father and of the Son and the Holy Spirit, teaching them to observe all that I have commanded you. And behold, I am with you always, to the end of the age."

REFLECTION QUESTIONS:

How can you, as a coach or leader, change your tone and your tongue?

What can you do to make your walk match your talk, as stated in Matthew 5:16?

What can you do to impact the officials and other teams so they can see Christ in your team and your staff?

PRAYER:

Lord, I know the Enemy is fighting to keep us distracted every day from the reason we coach. Would you please cover the readers and their teams with your presence? Make your presence so obvious that disdain and hatred cannot dwell in their souls. We honor You in everything we do. Thank you for the hedge of protection around the readers, authors, and their families. In Jesus name, Amen.

RESPOND:

Write down your own thoughts, observations, application points and/or prayers.

_____

_____

_____

_____

_____

_____

_____

_____

_____

_____

_____

_____

_____

_____

_____

_____

_____

_____

_____

_____

_____

_____

_____

PROVERBS 26

VERNON FOX III
Retired NFL Player, Former High School Coach, Speaker, Author, Minister
Las Vegas, NV

KEY VERSE: v.13-15

THE SLUGGARD SAYS, 'THERE IS A LION IN THE ROAD! THERE IS A LION IN THE STREETS!' AS A DOOR TURNS ON ITS HINGES, SO DOES A SLUGGARD ON HIS BED. THE SLUGGARD BURIES HIS HAND IN THE DISH; IT WEARS HIM OUT TO BRING IT BACK TO HIS MOUTH.

As coaches we are often tasked with bringing the best and most out of those in whom we lead. While talent, skill, and natural ability all play a part in getting people to produce results, there have always been intangible attributes that can never be coached. One's willingness, determination, drive, and effort have all forever proven to be the difference between those that are effective and those that are not. Proverbs speaks of "the sluggard." This is the one who would rather choose fear over courage, rest over work, and laziness over effort.

If we study the Word of God, we will learn that faith is one of the strongest attributes of believers. In James 2:17 we learn that in order for faith to be activated, true faith is something that must be coupled with action. This is the exact opposite of what we see from the sluggard. The sluggard's plea of danger as described through the possibility of a ferocious lion lingering nearby is nothing more than an excuse to remain in fear and to avoid taking action. How often have we allowed excuses that were scapegoats and justifications for sluggard mentalities? We have watched even those with talent waste away, unwilling to work and exercise the effort needed to be anything more than mediocre.

I find it interesting that Solomon describes this character as one who rolls around in bed while others are practicing the daily habits that lead to success both naturally and spiritually. The spiritual health of the believer is predicated on our willingness to seek God with intentional effort and relentless pursuit. There is no time to lay on the figurative sidelines of life hoping that change takes place. When we remain in this place too long, we become lazy and lose the motivation to believe for anything more than what we become accustomed to. There is a sense of complacency that falls on those that adopt this mindset. It is in this place that the enemy can trick us into believing that there is no hope for us to be anything other than what we experience from this broken place.

As a coach, it is our job to help guide the sluggard out of this place that keeps them bound. To push them to understand that they can lean on us when they have nothing inside of them to push themselves. This is the image that God wants us to gather as well. His desire is that our dependance would be on Him and not ourselves. Our limited and inconsistent abilities will only take us so far, even when we have loads of talent and skill. The sluggard learns that it is more about a mindset than it is about a skillset. They learn that true change and transformation happens when we allow the power of God's Word to renew our minds and change us from the sluggard mentality. Coach, a large part of your responsibility is to direct the sluggard to God's Word and be the example through your everyday actions and speech. Be the change! Produce the change!

REFLECTION QUESTIONS:

Can you list out attributes and qualities of one who is opposite of the sluggard as described in Proverbs 26:13-15?

What are ways as a coach that you could push the sluggard outside of their comfort zone to be more productive?

Have you yourself struggled with symptoms of the sluggard? If so, what can you do to change that today?

PRAYER:

Heavenly Father, I realize that at times I can resemble the sluggard. It is hard for me to impact anyone and guide them away from character traits that I myself carry. I ask that you would first help me to battle against fearful, lazy, and effortless actions that hinder my life and effectiveness as a leader, and then help me to guide those that I impact away from the same. In Jesus' name, Amen.

RESPOND:

Write down your own thoughts, observations, application points and/or prayers.

_____

_____

_____

_____

_____

_____

_____

_____

_____

_____

_____

_____

_____

_____

_____

_____

_____

_____

_____

_____

_____

_____

_____

_____

PROVERBS 27

RYAN ROECKER

Athletic Director/Head Football Coach — Brazos High School
Wallis, TX

KEY VERSE: v.17

IRON SHARPENS IRON, AND ONE MAN
SHARPENS ANOTHER.

This is a verse that has had a great meaning to my life for a long, long time. I was blessed to grow up in the church. It is there that I was formed a close relationship with a specific group of guys and they have provided important accountability over the years. We are not called to take this journey alone and I am so thankful for all the blessings I have received as a result of having these guys around me. Later, as my career developed, this verse continued to take on more meaning to me. Speaking to my Sunday school class this morning, we were talking about wisdom and accountability and I gave them this example:

Every summer we have workouts with our athletes. And every summer I have athletes miss workouts but tell me they are doing their workouts at home. They may be actually doing it but they are missing the point. The workout is just the small part; the large point is the accountability of us being together. Learning to sharpen either other through the easy things such as athletics allows us to build relationships that will allow us to sharpen each other in the tough things like life and our Christian walk. It's easy to tell a brother he missed a rep but it's a whole lot harder to call him out on a sin. If we do not spend quality time with one another, then we will not be able to speak truth into the lives of others. It is also easier for a major flaw or an unrepentant sin to go on festering if you do not have people who are walking with you in the everyday activities of life.

Here, in this verse God chose to use the word iron because when the tough things need to be called out it will stand. Imagine trying to go to war with a sword made of styrofoam. Or imagine trying use a piece of straw to hammer and forge an instrument made of iron. Thus, this verse goes both ways. In order to provide sharpening, long-lasting impact on the lives of those around you, you must be strong yourself. Yet one of the ways that we become strong, toughened, and sharpened, is to have others around us that truly bring out the best in us. That's why you want to have accountability built by iron. Don't try to do this walk alone. If you do not have someone like this in your life, pray about it and search out a brother.

REFLECTION QUESTIONS:

Do you have people in your life that sharpen you?

How can you continue developing relationships with others so that you can strengthen one another all the more?

How can you pray for others today?

PRAYER:

Lord, help me to daily look to you. I know you are the one who truly strengthens and sharpens me. I need you in my life so I can be strong. I also know that you carry out your work through others. Help me to be in close relationship with others who can shape me into something better. Help me to have a listening ear.

RESPOND:

Write down your own thoughts, observations, application points and/or prayers.

_____

_____

_____

_____

_____

_____

_____

_____

_____

_____

_____

_____

_____

_____

_____

_____

_____

_____

_____

_____

_____

_____

_____

_____

_____

PROVERBS 28

SPENCER CRACE
Offensive Coordinator/Area Director, FCA — Pacific Lutheran University
Tacoma, WA

KEY VERSE: v.1, v.5, v.26

THE WICKED FLEE WHEN NO ONE PURSUES, BUT THE RIGHTEOUS ARE BOLD AS A LION.

EVIL MEN DO NOT UNDERSTAND JUSTICE, BUT THOSE WHO SEEK THE LORD UNDERSTAND IT COMPLETELY.

WHOEVER TRUSTS IN HIS OWN MIND IS A FOOL, BUT HE WHO WALKS IN WISDOM WILL BE DELIVERED.

Have you ever felt that feeling of looking over your shoulder and just wondering who's watching? Or just wondering when your sin, your pain, your struggles, and your guilt are all going to catch up to you? You think the world is out to get you. So, what happens? You flee, you fall deeper into the pit more and more. The reality of all this is you have been captivated by fear, losing sight of the Holy Spirit, who is coming after your heart. But the righteous are BOLD as a lion. They never waiver or dwell in fear. They don't spend their days looking over their shoulder running from something that really isn't there. They live with peace in their heart and a boldness to proclaim the gospel. The righteous stand firm and never flee.

Today's world is captivated by fear. The media, gossip, and the need to be heard has filled our thoughts and our phones. Our world is full of injustices. We see them taking place all around us. We thrive for answers. We shout from the rooftops to stand for the oppressed. It is beautiful and I believe it is what Jesus would be doing right now. But we must remember that Jesus wouldn't be seeking recognition. He wouldn't try to be the loudest or have the greatest, well thought-out tweets. He would be listening, praying, loving, and serving. When our heart isn't in alignment with Jesus, we lose sight and understanding of justice. But when we STOP and seek the Lord, we begin to understand it completely! We begin to see the injustice through the eyes of Christ. Our world needs us seeking Jesus first, so we can then take on the calling to seek justice for the oppressed and the hurting, and thus we can run into the face of the storm as bold as a lion.

So, know this: we are nothing without Jesus. We could be an expert in our field, and even have a Ph.D. next to our name. We could be seen as a leader and be preaching from the pulpit. But, often times through notoriety and recognition we get lost in our own pride and fall victim to our own mind. A worldly mind will tell you that the more pats on the back, the better you are doing. But at some point, the pats on the back will come to an end... then what? We should be bold as a lion when seeking righteousness.

We must first stop and see the injustice of our world through the eyes of Jesus, asking for the Holy Spirit to transform our hearts and minds into game changers. We must seek the Holy Spirit whole-heartedly and pray to be filled with wisdom, peace, and understanding so we can do what Jesus called us to do. The time is now to seek wisdom and understanding and stand fearless with an abundance of boldness and with a hope that we will receive one pat on the back, and that's a pat coming from nail-scarred hands.

REFLECTION QUESTIONS:

What fears, guilt, and sins are causing you to look over your shoulder, prohibiting you from living a life of righteousness that is bold as a lion?

What are ways you seek to understand justice? What needs to change or are you doing really well in this area?

Luke 2:52 says, "Jesus increased in wisdom and in stature and in favor with God and man." How are you continuing to increase in wisdom? Have you fallen into the trap of your own thinking? What do you do to get out of that trap?

PRAYER:

Jesus, we thank you for coming after us! Your love is enough. Father, we pray that we can live in a way that seeks the applause of nail scarred hands. Give us strength to live a life of righteousness that is as bold as a lion. Fill our heart and minds with your Holy Spirt and help us understand more clearly the injustice and justice of our world. And Father, we pray that we can continue to seek wisdom and escape the trap of our own mind, pursuing a mind that is focused on knowing You more. We love You and praise You! Amen.

RESPOND:

Write down your own thoughts, observations, application points and/or prayers.

_____

_____

_____

_____

_____

_____

_____

_____

_____

_____

_____

_____

_____

_____

_____

_____

_____

_____

_____

_____

_____

_____

_____

_____

_____

PROVERBS 29

ALEX JOHNSON
Activities Director — Clinton High School
Clinton, MO

KEY VERSE: v.1, 9-10

HE WHO IS OFTEN REPROVED, YET STIFFENS
HIS NECK, WILL SUDDENLY BE BROKEN BEYOND
HEALING.

IF A WISE MAN HAS AN ARGUMENT WITH A FOOL,
THE FOOL ONLY RAGES AND LAUGHS, AND THERE
IS NO QUIET.

BLOODTHIRSTY MEN HATE ONE WHO IS BLAMELESS
AND SEEK THE LIFE OF THE UPRIGHT.

We have all been there. You are the new coach in town. As
you begin working with the new program, you start building
relationships with teachers, administrators, parents and fellow
coaches who you think have your best interest at heart. You
dive in head first because of course "it's all about the kids." You
are fired up for this new journey, and rightfully so. You come
home from practice and all you can talk about is your new job.
Conversations turn into thoughtful, in-depth questions and
the small, still voice of discernment (your wife, friends, family,
etc.), offers up some wisdom. That voice tries to warn you to
"be cautious" and not dive in headfirst to new friendships and
relationships without using discernment. You want to remain a
trusting person though, so you think, "no, they would never hurt
me..."

Fast forward and you are stuck wishing you would have listened.
Sound familiar? This is the story of many coaches and it happens
to be my own personal journey which I have walked through

during my young career. I still remember getting that first job offer. It was great. My wife and I spent our first three years of marriage in a small town. I taught every kid K-12 in the PE Classroom, coached football, basketball, and track and we became part of the very fiber of the community. Three years in, however, the grass was looking a little greener in Texas and my wife and I picked up and moved for a 6A job in the Dallas-Fort Worth Area. Honestly, those formative years had their struggles, but I never truly "got burned." It was a great community. The kids were buying in. We had developed life-long friendships, and God was truly using us. Looking back now, however, I wonder if that greener grass was really that green at all.

Fast forward to our time in Texas. For all intents and purposes, things were going great. I was working long hours as the middle school "grinder." No job was too small for me, as I was "working my way up in the system." Coaches at the varsity level were telling me how excited they were to have me up on staff. I even landed a Special Teams Quality Control Position and was transitioning to a more inclusive role with the varsity. Then, it happened. The proverbial door was shut on our time in Texas, and in a way that I definitely did not see coming. Again, everything looked like it was going "great," from the outside. But without warning, it was time to move on. As I sat home reflecting while also stressing over what was next, I wondered, had I listened to that small, still voice? I asked myself what I could have done differently. How did I end up here? Silence... or so I thought. Well, when one door closes...

My wife and I quickly picked up our now growing family and headed back to New Mexico. I jumped right into coaching. I was involved in cross country, football, basketball, and track. December rolled around and the AD position opened up. I took it without hesitation and thought, "okay God. I see it now." Then, as so often happens, life sped up. With all the success I was having personally in my career, however, I was convinced that God was blessing every decision I was making. How could I see it any other way? The proof was in the proverbial pudding. The only problem, though, was again, that small, still voice (my wife) was warning me and I have to say, I was not doing a good job of listening. Entering year three, things still appeared "great" from the outside looking in. I had moved up the ladder into administration, I finally felt like I had a grip on the AD role, and our programs had reached levels of success not previously seen in the district. I started working on a character curriculum with a close friend and fellow "culture builder," and I presented it to the school board for review. We were going to implement this thing from the top down in the athletic department. I was so excited. After that board meeting, however, the same people who I had leaned on, trusted, and worked with during my first two years in the district quickly decided that I did not fit their plans.

My job was protested at Central Office. I was even told that I should consider resigning my position for the "greater good." It was happening again. I thought, "no, no, no, this cannot be happening." Over the course of the next several months, I opened up my ears again to that small, still voice. We as a family endured what I would say was the most trying time in my career. Looking back, I see Proverbs 29 as God's wake-up call in my life. How many times had God attempted to get my attention? What was it going to take for me to "unstiffen" my neck and listen? In spite of these trials, however, I believe that God showed up in a mighty, revealing to me these simple truths.

Don't wait to listen before it's too late and you are left in a state that is "beyond healing." Some people are simply not on your team and they never will be. Be okay with this. Walk in righteousness. "Shake the dust" in God's timing. Sometimes when you are being attacked, understand that it may not be you. Again, not everyone is on your team and the enemy will try to break you with these people. Don't let him! Find your hope in the Lord and "he will make your paths straight."

REFLECTION QUESTIONS:

Are you listening to the small, still voice which is trying to save you from your own demise?

Are you using discernment when it comes to who you allow in your "circle?"

PRAYER:

Lord help me to use discernment in everything I do. God, when I am not listening, open my eyes to the people and circumstances who will allow me to let down my walls and be open to YOUR Spirit moving in my life. Lord, I pray for those who wish harm on me and want to see me fall. Help me be okay with those who don't want to "get on my bus." I love you Lord. Guide me. Lead me. Remind me you are always here.

RESPOND:

Write down your own thoughts, observations, application points and/or prayers.

_____

_____

_____

_____

_____

_____

_____

_____

_____

_____

_____

_____

_____

_____

_____

_____

_____

_____

_____

_____

_____

_____

PROVERBS 30

RAMONE CONLEY
Assistant Football Coach — Fairfield Christian Academy
South Bloomfield, OH

KEY VERSE: v.5, v.7-9, v.11-14

EVERY WORD OF GOD PROVES TRUE; HE IS A
SHIELD TO THOSE WHO TAKE REFUGE IN HIM.

TWO THINGS I ASK OF YOU; DENY THEM NOT
TO ME BEFORE I DIE: REMOVE FAR FROM ME
FALSEHOOD AND LYING; GIVE ME NEITHER
POVERTY NOR RICHES; FEED ME WITH THE FOOD
THAT IS NEEDFUL FOR ME, LEST I BE FULL AND
DENY YOU AND SAY, 'WHO IS THE LORD?' OR LEST
I BE POOR AND STEAL AND PROFANE THE NAME OF
MY GOD.

THERE ARE THOSE WHO CURSE THEIR FATHERS
AND DO NOT BLESS THEIR MOTHERS. THERE ARE
THOSE WHO ARE CLEAN IN THEIR OWN EYES BUT
ARE NOT WASHED OF THEIR FILTH. THERE ARE
THOSE—HOW LOFTY ARE THEIR EYES, HOW HIGH
THEIR EYELIDS LIFT! THERE ARE THOSE WHOSE
TEETH ARE SWORDS, WHOSE FANGS ARE KNIVES,
TO DEVOUR THE POOR FROM OFF THE EARTH, THE
NEEDY FROM AMONG MANKIND.

As you read through this Proverb, which was written by a wise
man named Agur, you see some things that truly stand out. Agur
speaks of leaning on God and not relying on self. This is huge in
today's society because we often lean on ourselves and only lean
on God when we need Him. We ask God for things over and over
for ourselves like He is a magical genie, instead of truly having
a relationship with Him. Agur speaks against this. Look at verse
5 when Agur says "He is a shield to those that take refuge in
Him." God will help in times of trouble and we should absolutely

lean on Him in those times, but having a relationship with Him and following His Word can help us avoid some of the strife and troubles we tend to get ourselves in. This verse is showing us that God gave His Word to be encouragement and wisdom to His people. It is on us to utilize that "shield" that God gave us.

Agur goes on in verses 7-9 to ask God to remove riches from his life so he will not ask "Who is the Lord?" which means he no longer needs God. He also asks that he not be poor, which may lead him to speak ill and curse against God. People often get complacent when everything is going right. They often forget to lean on God and continue that relationship. Why would I need God when I am the one being successful? It goes the same way for when we are completely struggling. Some of us lean on Him in these times but some of us start getting angry at God and cursing His name. We often blame Him when we are at the lowest. *How could you let this happen to me God? If you are so mighty and powerful, why would you allow this to happen to me?* This goes back to Agur knowing that leaning on God is important in all situations, the good and the bad, the ups and the downs, which is something society as a whole, and even myself at times, struggles to comprehend.

Another theme that Agur addresses throughout this Proverb is the theme of society not following God's Word. Wow, is that not true for the society we are currently living in? He talks about folks cursing their mothers and fathers, something God speaks very highly of and of course we know was a commandment of God. He goes on to talk about a generation of folks that are "pure in their own eyes but are not washed of their filth." He is speaking of people that believe they are sinless or are sinning but are covering it up. When we ignore or cover up our sin, it leads to destruction. This verse goes on to talk about folks who "lofty are their eyes and how high their eyelids lift." This is referring to pride and being prideful. Which at times, we as coaches and people all can be. Especially when things are going right and we are being successful. He finally finishes up talking about greed and how the greedy try to devour. Man, this one stings for me because it's speaking of trying to become greedy in everything we want instead of cherishing what God has for us right where we are. The proverb finishes up talking about some of the other things that tend to get people in trouble because of their lack of a relationship with the Father. It talks about mocking others, adultery, hatefulness, trying to be overly wise (wiser than the Father).

But all is not bad. This Proverb is trying to get us as people and a society to lean more on Him. To follow the Word of God. To love His people and treat them with respect and honor. To follow the commandments. People that do these things are wise and will lead to a life of blessings. Tough times will still come, but we will have a shield to help take refuge in. HE IS OUR SHIELD.

REFLECTION QUESTIONS:

Think about things in your life that can be a detriment to God.

Has there been a time recently that you were prideful and arrogant?

Has there been a time recently when you have become complacent and forgot to work on that relationship with God?

Has there been a time recently when you haven't followed his commandments or have struggled to follow them?

PRAYER:

Dear Heavenly Father, I come to you asking you to search my heart and help me to locate anything detrimental of you, anything that Agur was speaking about that can hurt my relationship with you. Heavenly father I want to thank you for your grace and mercy, especially in times like this whenever I fall short and you still forgive me and help our relationship grow. I am thankful for your mercy and grace. Continue to help me grow and separate myself from the things spoken of in these Proverbs. Help me live the way you want me to live, help me to shine YOUR light in all circumstances. In Jesus' heavenly name I pray, Amen.

RESPOND:

Write down your own thoughts, observations, application points and/or prayers.

_____

_____

_____

_____

_____

_____

_____

_____

_____

_____

_____

_____

_____

_____

_____

_____

_____

_____

_____

_____

_____

_____

_____

_____

PROVERBS 31

TOMMY POYNTER
Athletic Director/Head Football Coach — Wills Point High School
Wills Point, TX

KEY VERSE: v.3

> DO NOT GIVE YOUR STRENGTH TO WOMEN, YOUR WAYS TO THOSE WHO DESTROY KINGS.

"Everybody wants to be head coach." We have all heard that saying before in coaching. Most of the time it is said when there are too many cooks in the kitchen, so to speak. Head coaching jobs are difficult to come by—especially football jobs. What should we do when we are in positions of leadership though? I know many assistants and coordinators who desire to become head coaches and when given that opportunity I have seen some of them fail because they decided to give their strength to ways "that destroys kings." There are many of those ways and they should be identified!

Proverbs is a book that issues great warnings. Proverbs 31:3 gives two warnings: to not give your strength to women and not to ways (or things) that destroy kings. What are those things? I believe drinking is one of them. For Christians, alcohol can be a touchy subject; how much is too much? Should Christians drink alcohol? I don't know the answer to that, but Proverbs does say strong drink is "a brawler" (20:1). There is a reason why they also call alcohol 'spirits.' Alcohol can take over your mind and your decision making! There are many more 'spirits' beyond drinking that could intoxicate a leader. The power of 'that chair' can also consume (or even overwhelm) you if you are not careful.

Personally, I cannot take a drink of alcohol without being totally convicted—nor can I swear, nor look at another woman lustfully without the Holy Spirit coming over me in conviction. It is an awesome place to be, totally controlled by the Holy Spirit, in which there is freedom to do anything. The Holy Spirit gives me the power to do more than I could ever imagine or ask (Ephesians 3:20-21) but also makes me meek.

Speaking of women, that verse says not to give your strength to women. What does that mean? Remember that Proverbs 5 makes it abundantly clear to not give yourself to a woman who is not your wife. The immoral woman leads to death! I believe Proverbs 31 is issuing the same warning. Instead, we ought to be looking for a woman who fears the Lord.

Verses 10 thru 31 of Proverbs 31 are the example we as men ought to be looking for in a wife: prudent, wise, discerning, bringing glory, strong, honoring to those around her. What great leadership qualities! Many of those qualities are the same qualities of Jesus. To find them in a wife is even more glorious! I'm thankful for my wife that God has blessed me with, Emily is a clear example that I have "outkicked my coverage" as they say. I believe God gave Emily to me as an example for how I am to act as an athletic director and head football coach! She is my spiritual sounding board. In fact, some of my own head coaching ideas have come straight from her. I believe the 'Proverbs 31 Woman' traits are the same traits we should have as head coaches!

I know if we are wanting to be used by God as a leader for his Kingdom, I think the amount of sacrifice required has to match the 'call' (or desire) we have to lead. I'm not saying a Christian should never drink, but if your body is a temple of the Holy Spirit and we have been bought at a price and we are commanded to honor God with our bodies (1 Corinthians 3:16, 6:18-20), then I think a Christian should consider if using alcohol is going to impact their witness to others around them. I truly desire my players to see me as the example. Some of my deepest regrets when I was a player were that I didn't fully realize how to use my body to honor the Lord.

117

I know that many believers battle with legalism, which Christ also died for (along with every other sin), and I have battled with it as well. If you struggle with legalism, remember that Philippians 2:12 tells us to "work out your own salvation with fear and trembling." This means you have the liberty to decide what you can allow into your life (1 Corinthians 10:23). I know many successful head coaches who are more liberal in what they do when it comes to alcohol.

Many people love Proverbs 31 because of how it describes a godly woman, and it truly does. Additionally, the woman or virtuous wife is who we are to be as the church of Jesus Christ! But let us not overlook the first 9 verses. I feel that true leadership is found in men who do not give themselves to alcohol, women, or other ways that destroy kings. They instead stand up for the ones who cannot speak for themselves, fight for the poor and the needy, and look to the Lord (and to their wives) as their source of power and inspiration. All Scripture is God-breathed, and Proverbs 31 is no exception!

REFLECTION QUESTIONS:

As a leader, to what do you ascribe your strength? Is it to the Lord? Is it something else?

Why do you think kings should open their mouths for the speechless? What does that look like for you as a coach?

How are we doing church? Do we meet the mark or miss it when we replace the 'virtuous wife' as the church that Christ died for?

PRAYER:

God, help me to find my strength in you and you alone. Let me not give my strength to other things, such as lusts of the flesh, the lust of the eyes or the pride of life. Father, help me to see what your church should really be like as the 'virtuous wife' in Proverbs 31! Let me run hard after you and listen to your word so that I may become the leader and coach that you truly desire. I trust you Jesus with my life, and I love you all the more. Amen.

RESPOND:

Write down your own thoughts, observations, application points and/or prayers.

_____

_____

_____

_____

_____

_____

_____

_____

_____

_____

_____

_____

_____

_____

_____

_____

_____

_____

_____

_____

_____

_____

_____

_____

_____

_____

_____

_____

Made in the USA
Middletown, DE
02 June 2022

66566117R00076